THE
PICTURE
ENCYCLOPEDIA
OF
SMALL
PLANTS

THE PICTURE
OF SMALL

ENCYCLOPEDIA PLANTS

Jack Kramer

Drawings by Robert Johnson

5D STEIN AND DAY/*Publishers*/New York

First published in 1978.
Copyright © 1978 by Jack Kramer

All rights reserved.
Designed by Barbara Huntley
Printed in the United States of America
Stein and Day/*Publishers*/Scarborough House,
Briarcliff Manor, N.Y. 10510

Library of Congress Cataloging in Publication Data

Kramer, Jack, 1927-
    The picture encyclopedia of small plants.

Includes index.
1. House plants—Dictionaries.   2. Miniature plants—Dictionaries.
I. Title.   II. Title: Small plants.
SB419.K723   635.9'65   78-1089
ISBN 0-8128-2497-0

All photos are by Matthew Barr unless otherwise attributed.

CONTENTS

THE
PICTURE
ENCYCLOPEDIA
OF
SMALL
PLANTS

CHAPTER ONE

Small Plants: Their Shapes, and Uses

Today we grow plants indoors more than ever, mainly because we yearn for some green accent, some living thing to complement our furnishings and brighten our existence. Because our indoor spaces are generally small, the plants we grow are proportionally small. Huge trees and large bushy plants that require lots of room are certainly seen decorating the expensive interiors shown in slick house and home magazines, but most of us need the little plants to satisfy our basic need for indoor greenery. Small plants are compact and attractive and after they've adjusted to your conditions they're easier to care for than their giant relatives. They can be true miniatures (2 to 6 inches tall), dwarfs (6 to 12 inches high), semidwarfs (to 14 inches high), or small plants (to 16 or 18 inches in height). The sizes given for these categories are approximate; it is to avoid the confusing technical differences that exist in the classification of small plants in catalog and flower shops. For convenience I have used the term "small plants" for all those in this book. Let me now introduce you to the enjoyable world of small plants.

A shelf arrangement is handsome in any room, and small plants are ideal for this indoor decoration. The small philodendrons on the lower shelf make a nice green accent. *(Photo courtesy of Potted Plant Information Center.)*

This lovely miniature orchid is *Dendrobium jenkensii. (Photo courtesy of American Orchid Society.)*

CATEGORIES

Miniatures

These lilliputians, found in such plant families as orchids, geraniums, begonias, cacti, and succulents, do not grow over 6 inches tall in cultivation. Most miniature plants are true from nature—not hybridized—but some, such as the miniatures from the Geranium, Saintpaulis, Peperomia, and Hedera families, have been hybridized. They are naturally small and grow slowly.

At first you will find that miniature plants require more adjustment than larger plants. A large plant can usually make the jump from greenhouse to your house in about one week; the tiny gems take at least a month. During that time you must give miniatures extra care, but after a month routine plant care is all that is needed. The actual potting of miniatures and the types of containers in which they should be planted deserve special consideration; you'll find that in Chapter 3.

Miniatures are truly ideal apartment plants, never cumbersome or hard to handle, never too demanding. If you do lose a plant along the way, it's not a catastrophe because miniatures cost less than large plants; in fact, many miniatures are *very* inexpensive.

Dwarfs and Semidwarfs

It's difficult to determine by exact size just which plants are dwarfs and semidwarfs. Classification by inches of height just does not seem to work very well, but many flower shows include these categories, so it's necessary to think about measurements. It is impractical to give specific size in inches because the growth of a plant depends on specific cultural conditions. Here, then, is a rule of thumb:

Dwarfs are varieties that do not grow over 12 inches. They can be kept to this height under conditions that restrict growth although they might grow somewhat larger if given the chance.

Semidwarf varieties can grow to 14 inches and stay within that limit for over a year.

Small Plants

Finally we come to small plants, and the line here is usually drawn at 20 inches. If grown very well, some of these could be considered standard plants.

It's probably best to save confusion and argument and just say that all these plants—miniatures, dwarfs, semidwarfs, and small plants—are just that—small plants. That is to say that they're smaller in size than standard houseplants. Remember though that in every case except the true miniatures, many of these plants could overlap categories and be reclassified. So let's forget about inches and concentrate on plants.

Bonsai

The true art of bonsai, growing dwarf trees in small containers, is a fascinating technique, but it requires infinite care and costly plants. Nevertheless, the art of growing small plants in bonsai fashion is very possible for the average indoor gardener and offers a great deal of beauty and fun. So while this book doesn't discuss *true* bonsai, the techniques that are here are certainly worthwhile and comprise still another satisfying area of growing small plants.

There are some plants in many plant families that are suitable for bonsai growing; these are the plants that have some unusual characteristic—perhaps a handsome branching habit or an unusual upright pattern. Even a small orange tree, properly shaped and trimmed, can be a candidate for bonsai culture.

With bonsai the container is as important as the plant, and each must complement the other to create the proper effect. A very fine porous soil is also necessary for growing small plants in trays and dishes. And of course caring for the plants demands proper watering and maintenance methods.

A small orange tree was used here in bonsai style to create a handsome decoration. The container is as beautiful as the plant.

LEAVES

It is almost impossible to classify all the different types and textures of leaves, so this will be a cursory look. Graceful scalloped or lobed leaves abound in the Begonia and Gesneriad families. Plants from the succulent families almost always have fleshy and oval, almost buttonlike, leaves closely set together. Fleshy heart-shaped and oval leaves appear in the Peperomia family, and Orchids and Bromeliads have lance-shaped or strap-type leaves. Indeed, a leaf is not just a leaf; each plant has distinctive leaves, and each type of leaf has a definite character. You'll want to consider leaf style when selecting your small plants.

Leaf Color

Green is not simply green; there are about a dozen variations of green. Small plants like African violets, for example, have dark green leaves, whereas plants like small Sedums and Echeverias have almost apple-green foliage. Some miniature Begonias have multicolored leaves, as do the exquisite Caladiums and Marantas.

Marantas are ideal small plants for desk or table decoration.

Mix plants with leaf color in mind. Use all one tone of green or a graduating scale of green, from dark to light, for a handsome effect. Be careful when choosing multicolored leaves because if you mix in one group plants with variegated leaves, the colors may sometimes clash.

Pay attention to plant and leaf shape and leaf color when you buy your plants. It takes a little longer to shop this way, but you'll have plants that really fit into your decor, and which won't look incongruous.

FLOWERS

Small plants can have incredibly large flowers, as evidenced by certain cacti and succulents. A parodia, for example, which is only 2 inches across, may have a flower 3 inches in diameter. And a 5-inch plant like the orchid *Trichopilia elegans* may have a 5-inch flower.

USES

Many small plants are used in terrariums; certainly the small ferns and peperomias owe their present popularity to the terrarium craze. Orchids have recently entered the domain of the living room because of their easy care and color. Small cacti and succulents have been favorite houseplants for years, especially in sunny rooms, because those plants don't need much water. Small plants have an extraordinary number of

Parodias are ideal cacti for small decoration, and they do flower indoors.

uses; just what you do with them depends on your own tastes. You can have a charming collection of little plants at little cost and with very little investment of time. That's one of the large dividends growing small plants pays.

Besides growing small plants in terrariums, you can grow them at your windows. Most windows can accommodate no more than three large plants, but you can grow as many as 20 small plants at one exposure and have a year-round garden to keep you in bright spirits.

Small plants create a handsome setting anyplace; here they decorate a dining room corner.

A beautiful dish garden is still another fine idea. In this sort of simulated landscape tiny ficus plants can masquerade as trees, and little ferns can furnish a graceful note. The many plants suitable for dish gardens are generally the same plants that are used in terrariums. Finally, the plant in a hanging container has taken the spotlight lately; small plants are quite suitable for hanging baskets. Tiny-leaved tradescantias, for example, make handsome vertical green columns indoors.

I hope that I've whetted your interest in the intriguing world of small plants. There's more useful information in Chapter 2 to guide you along the way.

Even two plants on an end table can create beauty. Here African violets set the scene.

CHAPTER TWO

Care of Small Plants

The initial care you give your houseplants is more important than later routine care because plants have to get off to a good start. Plants you buy have been growing in more or less controlled environments, so their transfer to your home is a shock for them. Adjustment is necessary, especially with small plants, because they're sometimes more temperamental than large ones. Adjustment involves (1) conditioning to the new environment, (2) repotting if necessary (and it usually is), and (3) a suitable place with appropriate light. These are the three concerns that will be covered here, along with tips on insect prevention and some other guidelines for good plant culture.

CONDITIONING

You dare not take your plants home and just set them in a sunny window; they've probably been growing in filtered light. Extreme direct sun at a window could kill your plants within 48 hours. The first thing to do then, when you get plants home, is to put them where they'll get some light, but not in a sunny place. The temperatures should be about 70 degrees during the day and 55 degrees at night. Try an unheated pantry or any room where the heat isn't on all the time.

Make sure the spot has good air circulation, and if all seems well with your plants after a few days—no falling leaves or limp growth—move the plants to permanent bright, airy locations. It will then take them approximately another week to adjust, so don't panic if they drop a few leaves.

Remember, too when you get plants home, to look at the undersides of leaves; that's where most insects hide. Cut away any dead leaves and weak stems with a sterile sharp knife. Another nifty precaution is to soak plants to the rim of the pot in a sink of water until bubbles appear on the surface of the soil; that'll help eliminate any pesty insects.

The first few weeks with you your plants *do* need extra attention, but you'll be happy you gave them the extra care. In the long run the plants will be healthier for it. Begin right and you'll be able to relax later.

SOIL

Years ago, bulk soil was used for plants because that was all that was available. Today, soil is offered commercially in sacks

Standard packaged potting soil is fine for most plants and can be purchased at nurseries.

or bags. The packaging, though, often makes it difficult to determine the texture, content, and smell of the soil. A good soil is porous and feels like a well done baked potato when you run your fingers through it; it also has a woodsy smell. Buying packaged soil can be confusing, too, because there are so many brand names. Yet packaged soil is here to stay; it's convenient and good brands contain adequate nutrients. Here are some tips to help you select soil:

· Squeeze the bag; it should be mealy and soft to the touch.
· Examine the color; it should be earthy brown-black.
· Read the contents on the bag to determine just what is in the soil. Avoid those with inert "fillers."
· Never buy a bag of soil that is caked.

In addition to what is termed "houseplant soil" and sold as such, special soils are marketed specifically for cacti, African violets, geraniums, and other plants. Don't waste money on these; a good basic houseplant soil is fine for all small plants other than orchids and bromeliads. These two are potted in fir bark that's also available in bags from suppliers.

Some gardeners add organic matter—compost, manure, and so forth—to packaged soil, but this really isn't necessary. A good packaged soil will have sufficient organic matter in it to provide adequate nutrients. Additions really aren't necessary unless you're using poor soil. Trial and error is the only sure guide when selecting packaged soil. Once you've found the brand that gives the best results, stick with it as you would with any other purchased product.

REPOTTING

Do you repot a plant when you get it home or leave it in the soil it came in? Usually it is impossible to know how long a plant has been in the original soil, what kind of soil was used (it could be a soilless mix, which requires constant feeding), or if the nutrients in the soil have been used up. That's why you should repot new plants.

Repotting is not all that tricky; use packaged soil, and work at a waist-high bench or table. To remove the plant from the old pot and soil, simply tap the edges of the pot against the table until the rootball is loose. Now grasp the plant by the collar with your fingers and gently tease it from the pot with the rootball as intact as possible. Crumble away the old soil and you are ready to repot.

If you are repotting in a new clay pot, soak the pot overnight so it will not absorb the water that the plant needs; if the pot is old, scour it to be sure it's clean. (More about containers in the next chapter.) Put drainage chips in the bottom of any pot; drainage chips may be broken-pot pieces or gravel. Use about 1 inch of chips to a 4-inch pot. Now put in some new soil and center the plant. Fill in and around the plant with fresh soil to one inch from the rim, and tamp the bottom of the pot on the table to settle the soil. Be sure to pot tightly, but not so tightly that the soil is compacted too much. Should you

REPOTTING PLANTS

Remove young plant from small container, remove old soil

Prepare 5″ pot with pot particles for drainage

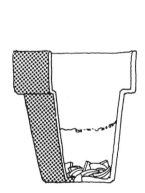

Add fresh soil

Place plant in pot and add soil

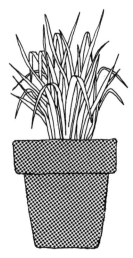

Pack soil and water copiously

need to repot again later, and find that a plant will not come out of its pot, break the pot rather than risk damaging the plant by tugging on it.

After you've repotted the plant, soak the soil until water runs out the drainage holes. Wait a few minutes, and then soak the soil again.

WATERING

Specific watering instructions are in the Picture Encyclopedia section but a more general discussion of watering will help you, too. Use tepid water, if possible; very cold water shocks some plants just as a cold shower would shock you. If you have a bucket or watering can, allow the water you'll use to stand overnight. That will allow it to reach room temperature, and also help to eliminate chlorine from the water.

When you water the plants, do it thoroughly. Scanty watering results in pockets of dry soil. When plant roots have to reach for moisture, that effort saps strength from the plant.

It's best to water plants in the morning and on bright days. Too much water on gray days can help to start fungus disease in some plants. If you're not sure your plants need water, it's better for them to be a bit dry rather than too wet. A very soggy soil can turn sour, and that can harm some varieties.

A good rule of green-thumb is to set up a watering schedule: approximately three times a week in spring and summer and twice a week in fall and once a week in winter. If there is a great deal of artificial heat, however, water more often. However, a specific watering schedule for *your plants* depends on the size of the pot the plants are in; how much artificial heat is used, and the general climate of your area. Watering plants properly takes some experience and after awhile you'll be able to determine if plants need water simply by looking at them—when leaves seem wan and limp, water is needed. Also remember soil in plastic pots retains moisture longer than soil in clay pots. Moisture will evaporate through a clay pot, but not a plastic one.

Some plants like to be evenly moist while others prefer to dry out between waterings; the Plant Encyclopedia will tell you which are which.

HUMIDITY

Humidity, the amount of moisture in the air, is an important consideration in growing plants indoors. While it is true that many plants do prefer relatively high humidity to grow well, most can adapt to less than optimum conditions if necessary. There are hundreds of plants that can grow in average home humidity which, in many parts of the country, is usually 20 to 40 percent. Very low humditiy (less than 15 percent) is detrimental to both plants and humans.

For plants that require higher humidity—gesneriads, for example—there are ways of furnishing additional moisture in the air. You can spray the plants with water once a day or even more often, especially when the weather is dry. You can also set potted plants on a bed of gravel in a planter. If you keep the gravel moist, evaporation will furnish some humidity in the growing area. Remember, too, that many plants growing in one area create their own humidity because they give off moisture through their leaves.

So there are ways of dealing with humidity for plants. Generally, remember that the hotter it is—summer, for example—the faster air dries out. Plants give off moisture faster when the air is dry than when it is damp. If they lose water quicker than they can replace it, their foliage becomes thin and depleted. Don't forget that in winter, when artificial heat is high, some additional moisture will also be needed in the growing area.

To measure moisture in the air, buy a hygrometer at a hardware store or nursery; this instrument tells you what you want to know in percentage figures. Remember that most plants will do fine with humidity in the 20 to 40 percent range.

PLACING PLANTS

Light is important to all plants, but a light, bright position does *not* mean sun. Direct sun, especially in the summer, can burn leaves, so it is much better to have plants in a bright place than risk leaf scorch. Any exposure is fine, contrary to popular opinion. True, flowering plants grow best in a south or east window, but foliage plants grow at any exposure. There are so many small plants suitable for east, west, and north light that you need never worry about exposure.

If you mean to worry anyhow, consider growing your small plants under artificial light. Read Chapter 5 for a good discussion of that subject.

PLANT FOODS

Plant foods fill nursery shelves in a bewildering array; there are liquid forms, granular types, foliar concoctions, and even chemical insecticides that include plant food in their formulations. Should you use plant food, and if so, which?

Remember that we want small plants to stay small; feeding them excessively will accelerate their growth. The answer to the feeding dilemma is to use plant foods, but in moderation. We do want our plants to be healthy, have strong stems, good foliage, and bloom well, so some feeding is fine.

I usually feed my plants once every month during spring, summer, and fall and not at all during the winter. You can modify this schedule somewhat, but only a little. Too much food can harm your plants if growing conditions are not perfect, and they rarely are indoors. Excessive feeding creates toxic salts in the soil which can rot roots. Take care when you feed that the soil is moist, and that the plants are in good health to start with. Never feed newly potted plants because they have enough nutrients in the soil to last them for at least six or seven months.

Plant foods have nitrogen to make leaves grow, phosphorous to stimulate good stem growth, and potassium to help make the plant strong. These elements are marked on the bottle or package in that order. For example, some plant foods are marked 10-10-5 which means they contain 10 percent nitrogen, 10 percent phosphorous and 5 percent potassium. The remainder is filler. For all practical purposes 10-10-5 is a fine all around feeding solution because it is neither too strong to cause leaf burn nor too weak to be effective.

Besides varying in percentages of elements, fertilizers also vary in form. Granular foods are scattered on plant soil, and then water is applied. This is a very convenient way to feed your plants. Soluble types are mixed with water and then applied to the soil. Foliar foods are also mixed with water but are sprayed on the leaves. Because many plants resent excess water on their leaves, it's usually best not to use foliar feeding. A new product called systemic fertilizer combines feeding and insect-control ingredients. I have not used it extensively, yet, so I can't make a recommendation.

Plant foods are necessary (unless you repot your plants frequently), so you should know how to use them to the best effect.

1. Never feed an ailing plant; it just cannot absorb the food.
2. Never feed plants when they are resting. Most plants do have an annual rest, generally in the winter.
3. Never try to force a plant into growth with excessive feeding; you will probably kill the plant.
4. Be sure the soil is moist before applying plant foods.
5. Do add some fish emulsion (sold at suppliers) about once every two months, and add some bone meal to flowering plants about once every two months.
6. Do not add compost to the soil.

7. When you use plant foods for a long period of time, toxic salts may build up within the soil. Flood the plant with water at the sink about twice a year. This leaching helps eliminate these salts.

INSECTS AND DISEASES

Small plants, like their larger cousins, will, occasionally, be attacked by insects, rarely by diseases. If you can catch insects before they get a foothold there is little problem in eliminating them. Even if they do get a head start there are ways to get rid of pests, but then the problem is more difficult. If you see insects on a plant, immediately remove it from the vicinity of other plants. That will help keep the infestation from spreading.

Keeping a plant in peak health is the best way to prevent problems because insects and attendant disease rarely attack healthy, well-established specimens. None of us is perfect, though, and occasionally our neglect allows insects to get a foothold or a disease to start. There's still no need to panic because there are ways to save your plant, often without extensive use of poisons. Merely hand picking insects can help a great deal. Grooming too—clipping off dead stems and leaves—is part of the preventative program.

Recognizing Symptoms

Before they become mortally ill, plants almost always reveal symptoms. Virus attacks are often an exception, though. But before you blame insects or disease, answer the following questions:

Is the plant getting too much or too little water?

Is the plant getting the right amount of food?

Is the plant getting too much or too little heat?

Is the plant getting too much or too little light?

Is the plant in a draft?

If the plant continues to fail, your first defense action is to observe the plant. Yellow or streaked leaves indicate something amiss, as do soft and brown stems. And foliage that just falls off is certainly a symptom of something awry, unless your plants are just going into their rest period.

There is absolutely no disease you cannot conquer if you catch it before it really becomes serious. If your culture is good and the plants still fail, then consider insects. Keeping your plants well-groomed is vital for their health. Spraying and misting leaves with tepid water goes a long way in preventing insects, because cleansing tends to remove insect eggs and spider mites before they hatch.

Leaf Conditions

A plant's leaves give many clues to its condition. A clean, healthy plant naturally has perky, fresh, green, good-looking foliage that is never discolored and streaked. Here are some unhealthy leaf conditions and their probable causes:

LEAF CONDITIONS	PROBABLE CAUSES
Brown or yellow areas	Incorrect feeding, sun scorch
Yellow or white spots	Leaf-spot disease
Leaf drop	Thrips, overwatering
Brown edges	Overwatering, salt damage
Curled	Salt damage, thrips
Dried and brown	Underwatering, not enough nutrients in soil
Leaves smaller than mature ones should be	Lack of nutrients
Sticky substance	Insects, usually aphids or mealybugs
Black sooty coating	Mildew
Silver streaked	Thrips
Eat n at edges	Slugs, snails
Coated white	Mildew and mold
Gray or yellow	Underfertilizing, mold
Deformed	Salt damage, mites
Transparent areas	Thrips

Stems and Crowns

Many fungus diseases start at the plant's collar. If caught quickly, they can be cured, but if neglected, these diseases can kill the plant. Many insects start their colonies in stems and leaf axils, so these are places to inspect very closely. Stems should be healthy and firm with good color; crowns of plants should be solid, never turgid or soft.

STEM AND CROWN SYMPTOMS	PROBABLE CAUSES
White or powdery stems	Mildew, mold
Limp stems	Overwatering, poor drainage
Stems covered with sugar substance	Ants which collect and gather colonies of aphids
Stems do not develop	Underfeeding or lack of water
Soft stem growth	Crown and stem rot disease, overwatering
Brown or gray crowns	Rot disease

INSECTS

Aphid

Mealy Bug

Scale

Thrip

Insects

Even with the best culture practices, plants will sometimes be attacked by insects. If you discover a light insect attack, don't worry about losing the plant; it can be saved by old-fashioned remedies, such as a laundry soap and water spray. The main thing, however, is to know what insect you are fighting before you do battle. Most of the common houseplant insects are recognizable on sight with a magnifying glass, including aphids, spider mites, mealybugs, scale, snails, and slugs. If you can't identify the insect, pick it off, kill it, and mail it to your County Agricultural Agent; he may be able to identify it. You'll find the address in your local telephone book.

APHIDS

An aphid is a pear-shaped, small, soft bodied insect with a beak that has four needlelike stylets. Aphids use these daggers to pierce plant tissue and suck out plant sap. These insects, sometimes called plant lice, can be green, black, red, yellow, or gray in color.

Aphids did some damage to this plant, and then snails moved in. Always keep plants free of insects.

Mealybugs can attack plants and harm them. When you see these white critters, use necessary precautions to protect your plants.

MEALYBUGS

Mealybugs have soft, segmented bodies dressed in cotton wax. They are oval-shaped, visible to the eye, and move slowly when they move at all. They have beaks to pierce plant tissue and suck out sap. Colonies are usually found in leaf axils.

RED SPIDER MITES

The true red spider mite that attacks plants is from the family *Tetranychidae*. These tiny oval creatures are hardly visible but they spin webs you may be able to see more easily. Mites injure plants by piercing the leaves and sucking liquid from the cells.

SCALE

Most often brown, scale are oval, tiny, but noticeable insects with an armored shell or scales covering their bodies. The insects suck plant sap and usually stay in the same spot on a plant's stem or leaves throughout their lives. Of all plant insects, scale is the easiest to recognize and combat.

THRIPS

Thrips are chewing, very small, slender insects with two pairs of narrow wings. Some thrips fly; others jump around. Their mouths are fitted with "tools" that enable them to pierce or rasp leaves. Adults are usually dark in color and most active between spring and summer.

Preventatives

Because there are so many insecticides and fungicides, it's essential that you know enough about them to avoid killing your plants with chemicals. Of course there's the question of whether or not you want to use poisons at all in the home since they can be a hazard. With that in mind I've also included some natural preventatives.

Chemicals to kill bugs come in several forms, but the granular type may be the most convenient to use. It is sprinkled on the soil and water is applied. Other chemicals are water soluble and are sprayed on plants. There are also powders and dusts, but these are probably best kept out of the home. Systemics are also popular. These granules are spread on the soil and then water is applied. Through the roots, the insecticide is drawn up into the sap stream, making it toxic to insects.

HOW TO USE CHEMICALS

No matter what poison you use, if any, do follow the directions on the package to the letter. In most cases repeated doses will be necessary to fully eliminate insects. Remember to keep the poisons out of reach of children and pets. Follow these rules when using chemicals:

1. Never use a chemical on a plant that is bone dry.
2. Never spray plants in direct sunlight.
3. Use sprays at the proper distance recommended on the package.
4. Try to douse insects directly if you can see them.
5. Don't use chemicals on ferns.
6. Always use chemicals in well-ventilated areas; outdoors is good.

Here is a list of chemicals, their uses, and some important things you should know about them.

TRADE OR BRAND NAME	PRINCIPLE USES	REMARKS
Malathion	Aphids, mites, scale	Broad spectrum insecticide fairly non-toxic to humans and animals
Sevin	General insect control	Available in powder or dusts
Meta-Systox	Effective on most but not all insects	Systemic; toxic but effective
Black Leaf 40	Aphids and sucking insects	Tobacco extract; relatively toxic but safe for plants.
Pyrethrum	Aphids, flies, household pests	Botanical insecticide; generally safe
Rotenone	Aphids, flies, household pests	Used in combination with pyrethrum
Aerosol bombs	Generally sold under different trade names as indoor plant sprays	Can harm leaves if sprayed too close; also can irritate lungs; do not use outdoor spray for indoor plants

TIME-HONORED REMEDIES

I have been gardening indoors for twenty years, long before modern insecticides hit the market, and I prefer the old-fashioned methods of eliminating insects from plants. They are perhaps not as thorough as chemicals, but they are safe and avoid noxious odors in the house.

Handpicking: Hardly pleasant, but it can be done with a toothpick.

Soap and water: For many insects, such as aphids and mealybugs, a solution of 1/2 pound of laundry soap (not detergent) and water works fine. Spray or douse the mixture on the bugs and repeat the applications every three to six days for three weeks.

Alcohol: Alcohol on cotton swabs will effectively remove mealybugs and aphids. Apply it directly to the insect.

Tobacco: A solution of old tobacco from cigarettes steeped in water for several days to get rid of scale. Repeat several times.

Water spray: This may sound ineffective, but it works if used frequently and with strong enough force to wash away insects.

Wipe leaves frequently: This simple step really goes a long way to reduce insect problems. It washes away eggs before they hatch.

Plant Diseases

Unfavorable growing conditions—too little or too much humidity, or too much feeding—can help to contribute to disease, but diseases are mainly caused by bacteria and fungi. Bacteria enter the plant through minute natural wounds and small openings. Inside, they multiply and break down plant tissue. Animals, soil, insects, water, and dust carry bacteria that can attack plants. And if you have touched a diseased plant, you too can carry the disease to healthy plants. Soft roots, leaf spots, wilts, and rots are some diseases caused by bacteria.

Fungi multiply rapidly in shady, damp conditions since moisture is essential in their reproduction. Fungi cause rusts, mildew, some leaf spot, and blights.

FUNGICIDES

Fungicides are chemicals that kill or inhibit the growth of bacteria and fungi. They come in dust form, ready to use, or in wettable powder. Soluble forms to mix with water and use as a spray are also available. The following is a brief resume of the many fungicides available:

Captan: An organic fungicide that is generally safe and effective for the control of many diseases.

Ferbam: A very effective fungicide against rusts.

Karanthane: Highly effective for many types of powdery mildew.

Sulfur: This is an old and inexpensive fungicide and still good; it controls many diseases.

Zineb: Used for many bacterial and fungus diseases.

Benomyl: A systemic used for many bacterial and fungus maladies.

As with all chemicals, use as directed on the package and with extreme caution. Keep all containers out of reach of children and pets.

CHAPTER THREE

Where to Put Plants, and in What

Chapter 1 briefly mentioned the many ways small plants can be used indoors; now let's explore these possibilities in detail: plants at windows, in terrariums, in dish gardens, in window and room greenhouses, and in hanging containers. We'll also consider just which containers are right for your plants. There are ornamental varieties, hanging pots, dish garden containers, and more. You'll want to become familiar with all types of containers so you can start right with your small plants.

WINDOWS

If you don't want plants cluttering up the house—and single pots of plants placed here and there can give a cluttered look—try a window garden. You can get perhaps twenty or thirty tiny gems in one window, and the plants will be easier to grow in that natural light than in any other place in your home. A few geraniums, a couple of orchids, and some miniature bulbs can dress up a window and your room considerably and take only minutes of care. Standard-size plants grow too large and awkward for most windows, but miniatures serve well.

The window garden brings the outdoors indoors, but a handsome window garden should not be just a haphazard arrangement. Group your plants with a design in mind. Mix branching plants with rosette types, follow the correct relationship of proportion and scale, and pay attention to color. A dark green plant, for example, next to a variegated one may look awful. It's easy to achieve the look you want, to blend small plants together properly so they create a unified composition. It's easy to do because the little fellows are lightweight and easy to move about.

Don't crowd plants at windows or they'll not have all the room they need to grow. Too many plants, one on top of another, looks straggly. Carefully select and mix and match to create a harmonious picture, or try using similar types of plants, all the same size. A window of cacti and succulents, for example, has appealing color and charm, and several small geraniums grouped together add a note of distinction.

The author's kitchen window houses many small plants. In the collection are ferns, philodendrons, chlorophytum, and other windowsill plants.

Here is a fine collection of
miniature gesneriads at this
window; note the
handsome scene it creates
in this areaway.

There are many plants and many arrangements to use at windows, and there are several ways you can accommodate the plants. Do you want one narrow planter at the window shelf, or do you prefer decorative containers? Do you want three or four glass shelves or hanging plants? Just remember that the window itself will often dictate the type of arrangement you should use. If you have a very wide window, for instance, most glass shelves are not sturdy enough to span the distance. If you are constantly using a window, nearby hanging plants may get in your way.

African violets are the star performers in this kitchen window scene. They offer color through the year.

Orchids and bromeliads occupy this garden room. At windows and spaced properly, they make a handsome scene.

Window Containers

CLAY POTS

Grandma used them, my mother used them, and I use them. I've tried other types of pots—plastic, acrylic, and so forth—but I always come back to the red terra-cotta pot, because it is serviceable, durable, and usually inexpensive compared to other pots. More important, to my way of thinking it is easier to judge when plants in clay pots need water—much easier

The selection of clay pots is vast. Choose the type you like for your plants.

than if they're in plastic pots. Lifting the clay pot is one way: if the pot is light, water is needed. Tapping the clay pot on its side is another way: if it rings hollow, water is needed.

Clay pots were once available in only a few sizes, but now suppliers sell many shapes and sizes. Here are some pots that are good for small plants.

Bulb pans or seed bowls are generally less than half as high as they are wide. They look like deep saucers but have drainage holes in them and are available in 6- to 12-inch diameters.

The azalea or fern pot, a squatty clay container formerly sold in only a few sizes, is now available in diameters from 6 to 14 inches. It is three-quarters as high as it is wide; that's a better proportion for most plants than conventional pots.

Three-legged pots are new and bring the bowl shape to the indoor garden. By raising the plants off a surface, these containers put the plants more on display. The pots range in size from 8 to 20 inches.

All new unglazed pots should be soaked overnight before they're used. Otherwise they'll absorb from the soil the water needed by the plants.

PLASTIC POTS

Plastic has come such a long way in the last decade that there are now many handsome plastic pots, but the watering of plants in plastic containers requires more attention than the watering of plants in clay pots. The plastic container has nonporous walls that prevent moisture from escaping. That means the soil stays moist longer than soil in clay pots. This can be an advantage or a disadvantage; sometimes—and it does happen—the soil becomes soggy because of too much moisture, and the plant is hurt. If you want to use plastic containers, you can certainly do so, but be forewarned that the plants in them need more care than plants in terra-cotta pots.

DECORATIVE POTS

There are many handsome and decorative plant containers—cachepots, novelty pots (crocks, teapots), glazed pots—that make stunning window decorations. But since most of them don't have drainage holes, watering a plant in one of those containers demands time, patience, and the ability to remember when you last watered. To use a cachepot or glazed pot correctly, you must plant in a clay pot and then put the clay pot inside the decorative container. When it's time to water, just remove the terra-cotta pot, returning it to its decorative container after excess water has drained out of the clay pot. Don't get carried away with ornamental containers. A few distinctive pieces are fine, but too many defeat the display purpose, and they are expensive.

Little novelty containers show off small plants delightfully, but because they're so small you cannot sit a clay pot inside them. Plant the novelty containers carefully, adding one teaspoon of charcoal chips to the soil, and make sure you do not overwater the container.

Window Greenhouses

These popular gardens give the apartment dweller a chance to have a stellar collection of almost any kind of small plants. The temperature, humidity, and air circulation conditions are near ideal because you can control them. Many plants such as the carnivorous types and the more delicate specimens like wildflowers, grow beautifully in greenhouses.

The small window greenhouse comes in many sizes and

Small plants are made for window greenhouses. In this homemade greenhouse there is a row of colorful African violets. *(Photo by Max Eckert.)*

styles; what you choose depends on your own situation. Generally, the window greenhouse is wood and glass, wood and acrylic, or aluminum framing with clear glass or acrylic panes. You can make your own window greenhouse—there are books on this—or buy a prefabricated kit and put it together yourself. The kits cost more than if you started from scratch, but they're less time-consuming.

TERRARIUMS

Terrariums—closed or semiclosed glass containers for plants—have become extremely popular in the last five years because they provide an ideal way of growing plants if you have little time to care for them. In a terrarium nature does the job for you. Plants transpire through their leaves, and this moisture collects on the walls of the container and drips down into the soil, constantly resupplying the plants with moisture. Temperature too is steady in the terrarium, so this method is an easy and happy way to grow plants.

Some terrariums are closed, that is, they have a lid or stopper or a pane of glass over the top. These closed cases rarely, if ever, require water. The open terrariums need some water, perhaps four times a year, but otherwise are almost as self-sufficient as closed cases.

This handsome terrarium has few plants but is still beautiful.

Start any terrarium right. Use a rich potting soil, and put a gravel bed about 1 inch deep in the bottom of the terrarium. The many facets of the stones help absorb any excess moisture that may accumulate on the bottom and sour the soil. Next add a handful of charcoal chips to help sweeten the soil. If possible, contour the soil with hills and valleys; that's better than a level soil line. This creates interest and enables plants to assume different roles, like trees or shrubs. The landscape may be a woodland, a seascape, or tropical in character. There are infinite ways to make terrarium landscapes, and there are an

A plastic dome terrarium is being prepared here. The plants include small gesneriads and ivy.

The terrarium being planted.

almost infinite number of plants to use in them to create that little spot of nature that can be so attractive in your home.

What to Use as Terrariums

Goldfish bowls, jars, empty water bottles, and all sorts of clear or stained glass or acrylic containers can be used for tiny plants; manufactured terrariums of assorted sizes and shapes (usually domes) are available. Anything you use as a terrarium should be leakproof, attractive, and not too large. For more information, read my book *The Complete Book of Terrarium Gardening* (New York: Scribner's, 1974).

A glass dome and a small decorative dish make a handsome indoor accent. Tiny plants are ideal for these gardens.

Dish gardens are old favorites and this one is a beauty. Note how the soil is formed into a hilly terrain. The plants include small ferns, hypoestes, and peperomia.

DISH GARDENS

The dish garden is similar to the terrarium, except that the plants grow in the open. The dish garden is a group of small plants designed and planted with originality. The plants and container should look like a single entity, so design is the foremost consideration. Never use too many plants in a dish garden; just a few is fine. You want a distinctive piece, not a jungle. Be sure that all the plants are in proportion to each other and that they harmonize. Choose one special plant and make it the focal point, the center of interest.

To start the dish garden right, prepare the soil base as you would for a terrarium. Now set plants *in their pots* into the dish and shift them around until they begin to look right to you. Moving them about will give you a chance to see how they interact with each other. Combine vertical with horizontal thrust, as well as leaf texture and color, so that the whole is a pleasing, eye-catching scene. Remember that dish gardens, like terrariums, are always on display.

Unlike terrariums, which can water themselves, dish gardens need routine plant care. Water your plants so the soil is evenly moist all year; this usually means watering every other day in hot weather. In winter you'll need to water them only about once a week, but the frequency depends on how much artificial heat you use indoors. If you use a great deal of heat, then you should give your plants more water to keep the humidity at a good level. Most plants get along fine with 20 to 30 percent humidity. Use a hygrometer in the growing area to determine humidity.

To pot a dish garden, remove the plants from the containers they were in when you got them at the store. Crumble away old soil and any excess roots that are brown at the tips. Dig shallow holes and spread out the roots of the plant; now add

Small bromeliads at the base of this dish garden offer year round color.

A dish garden (below) that uses miniature orchids and African violets creates a handsome scene and can be used for accent in any room.

fresh soil and pack it down around the collar of the plant. Finally, water the plants.

Just as before, be sure to occasionally wipe the leaves with a damp cloth to keep them clean and shiny and to help control insects that often accumulate at the bottom of leaves.

Dish Garden Containers

A dish garden container should be of a size, texture, and color appropriate to the mood you want to evoke with the plants you're growing. There are many suitable dish garden pots—most are shallow and resemble bonsai pots—in many shapes and sizes. The shallow pot gives the dish garden the proper frame, and the brown glazed containers are quite handsome. These are clay pots, so moisture evaporates slowly. The glazed bonsai pots are very nice, too, but with them you have a watering problem. A glazed container has nonporous walls, like a plastic pot, so moisture can't escape. Careful watering is the solution, but of course that can be a chore.

This dish garden has a diminuitive Christmas cactus in the background and a philodendron in the front; the dish used is a bonsai-type container.

A hanging garden with peperomias.

HANGING PLANTS

Growing plants in hanging containers has become justifiably popular because the plants are easy to see at eye level and they dress up otherwise useless space. Tradescantias, schizocentrons, and peperomias are perfect small hanging plants. They can be grown in a 6-inch pot; their stems may cascade 12 to 20 inches.

Be sure to hang your plants neither too high nor too low. You do not want them to obstruct traffic, nor do you want them so close to the ceiling that you have to make an effort to look at them. As a rule of thumb many people hang their plants at what would be the eye level of a 6-foot person.

Pot hanging plants as you do standard houseplants. If you want a quick rush of color, use two or three plants to a pot, positioning them in a triangular pattern. Be sure the plants get enough light. The picture encyclopedia that makes up the biggest part of this book lists dozens of plants suitable for hanging displays.

Chlorophytums are
handsome hanging plants
and can be used in
many areas.

Hanging
Containers

There are so many hanging containers that you'll have a hard time making your selection. Generally speaking, the plainer and more functional the container, the better. Baskets and macramé containers are striking, but water can rot the material. Make sure any hanging pot you choose has a built-in drip saucer because it is bothersome, to say the least, to have water dripping on the floors, or to have to carry plants to the sink for every watering.

Be sure you have suitable hanging hardware for your plants—chain or heavy-duty wire. The S-hooks you carefully put into the ceiling should always be screwed into a stud so that the hook doesn't become loose. Remember that a hanging plant, especially when watered, can be quite heavy: a 5-inch pot with soil, when wet, can weigh as much as 60 pounds!

CHAPTER FOUR

Getting Small Plants

Most plants are bought from plant stores or nurseries, and these outlets usually have a large, fairly inexpensive selection of small plants in 2- or 3-inch pots. What you can buy depends, of course, on what the dealer carries, but if you want one of the plants mentioned in this book and the dealer hasn't got it, you can order from one of the many mail-order suppliers located throughout the country. You'll find a list of such suppliers at the end of this book. You can also get new small plants by taking offshoots from suitable plants such as bromeliads and orchids that already belong to you or your friends. Some mature small plants can even be divided into several plants.

NURSERIES AND FLORISTS' SHOPS

Don't confuse a nursery with a wholesale outlet; they're entirely different. The former is what you want; it's usually not too far from any large city and is a good place to buy houseplants. A nursery has an incredible assortment of plants.

48

The stock in nurseries is usually very good and the turnover is fast, so you run very little risk of getting a bad plant. Florists' shops are fine for expensive dish gardens or terrariums you plan to give as gifts, but you should avoid buying your own plants there, unless you want to spend money. Florists do not carry many small plants, but those they do are of consistently top quality.

PATIO/GARDEN CENTERS; PLANT DEPARTMENTS; DISCOUNT STORES

The patio/garden centers usually charge somewhat higher prices than do large nurseries because these large complexes often pay high rents. Their stock is good, though.

Plant departments of large department stores like Montgomery Ward and Sears Roebuck and Company carry a large selection of small plants. The plants are usually of good quality and turnover is fast, so your chances of getting a bad plant here are slight, too. Their prices may be high, however, except during the sales that occur several times a year. Ads will tell you when. Bear in mind though that department store help frequently doesn't water or care for plants regularly, causing many good plants to die from neglect. Finally, in most of these departments the garden help and advice is anything but good, so you are more or less on your own. In other words, you will have to know something about plants to get the most for your money.

Episcias are ideal small plants for spot decoration on table or desk.

Woolworth's and other five-and-ten and discount stores have house and garden plant sections that carry various small plants at reasonable prices. These stores are good places for frugal shoppers, even though the plants may not be in tip-top shape. In such stores, as in plant departments, employees are often so busy that it may be impossible for them to water plants carefully and regularly. In those instances good plants can become bad ones in a few days' time. Try to get to the store the day the plant shipment arrives (usually on Thursdays or Fridays, although this varies from city to city) to get plants that are fresh.

HOUSEPLANT STORES

Between the fine florist shop and the old-fashioned nursery is a new category: the houseplant store and boutique. The merchandise here includes containers, terrariums, and odd-ments, as well as plants. The stores I have scouted have turned out to be excellent places to buy small houseplants, and sometimes they stock hard-to-find plants. The owners of these places are generally more interested in plants than are the larger concerns, whose buyers may each have several depart-ments to care for. With rare exceptions, the plant store owner knows plants by name and knows how to care for them. And the markup is rarely more than 25 percent, so you can get a lot for your money. Occasionally, if the store has only one plant of

A lovely crassula in a pretty pot makes a handsome window plant. *(Photo courtesy of Merry Gardens.)*

a kind, and you express interest in it, don't be surprised if you get a free cutting. That's *not* common practice, but now and then it does happen!

MAIL ORDER

Mail-order plant suppliers sell an astounding variety of plants and give some sound garden information in their catalogues. Some mail-order suppliers specialize in orchids, others stress annuals and perennials, and some feature indoor plants. There are many suppliers of *small* plants, and such specialization is fortunate because a specialist in one particular plant family is more apt to know plants as individual things of beauty rather than as commodities to sell. The seller's interest is to your benefit when you buy.

For years I have bought small plants from various mail-order companies, and I've been well pleased 99 percent of the time. But before you buy anything, write for the suppliers' catalogues. Some of them are free; few cost more than a dollar.

Some mail-order companies' catalogues can make a real gardener out of someone who's never grown plants before. The color photographs are incredibly beautiful, and frequently there is good advice and information about the wide array of plants offered. You can almost expect to be given the botanical names and cultivation guidance, for example.

Most mail-order plant suppliers are reputable and give you your money's worth. However, as with all businesses, there are some suppliers who don't deliver what they promise. The small-plant suppliers listed at the end of this book have all proven to be quite reputable.

Shipping Plants

What's the best method of transportation to get plants from mail-order suppliers to your home? You can leave this decision to the supplier, but then delivery will not be made the fastest way.

There are many ways to ship plants; it's worthwhile to investigate them all if you want fast service. There are also many different prices, so check things out carefully.

If you're in no great rush, have the plants shipped parcel post, the least expensive way. Pay a bit more and get parcel post-special handling, which will expedite the shipment. Air mail is expensive but does bring the plants to you overnight, or the second day at the latest. Check with your local post office about box-size limitations.

When you plan to receive *many* plants, Air Freight Collect is often advisible. Rates are based on a minimum of 100 pounds, so whether you ship 10 pounds or 100, the price is the same. For example, from Illinois to California the rate is about $19 per 100 pounds, and delivery is overnight. There is an extra charge for truck service from the airport to your home; I pick up my own plants to save this fee. On air freight shipments have the supplier include your phone number on the outside of the package so you can be called when the plants arrive.

A reasonably priced shipping service is Greyhound or Continental Trailways bus lines, if they operate within your area. This takes longer than other means of shipping, and you must pick up plants at the nearest station, but it is cheaper than Air Freight or Railway Express.

United Parcel Service (UPS) limits box size to 108 inches (length plus girth combined), but the rates are relatively moderate and service excellent.

Suppliers usually pack plants with sufficient care to protect them from heat and cold. If your plants do arrive in bad shape, notify the supplier at once. If you wait, your claim may not be honored.

PLANTS FOR FREE

The demand for plants has risen, and so have plant prices. You can save money by starting your own small plants from seeds or by the asexual methods of using cuttings and divisions. As a bonus, you can grow what you want rather than having to buy whatever plants are available at stores or nurseries.

Seeds

Mail-order suppliers sell the seeds of many varieties of houseplants. Start seeds in shallow pans or clay pots or any household container that is 3 to 4 inches deep and has drainage holes. Don't start too many seeds in the same container or you'll end up with a jungle.

Sow seed on a suitable sterile growing medium sold at nurseries. Sow most seed about 1/4 to 1/2 inch apart. Cover large- and medium-sized seed with a layer of dry mix; the layer should be twice the thickness of the seed. If the seed is very fine, merely scatter it on the surface of the soil. Now wet the seed bed so that it is uniformly moist. You can do that by misting the medium or watering from the bottom of the container. Now put water in a tray and place the tray under the container. To ensure good humidity, which seed need to germinate, prop four sticks in the container and cover them with a plastic bag. If too much condensation forms on the plastic, remove the bag for a few hours each day. Keep seed trays at an average temperature of 78°F. They should have light, but be out of the direct rays of the sun.

Germination time varies depending on the species; some seeds sprout in a few days, others take weeks, and some even take months. Once true leaves form and your plants have grown a few inches, remove the plants from their container

Seed kits (above) are available from many suppliers and offer a fine way to start your own plants.

This seedling is ready for a separate pot.

and plant them in soil in separate pots. For the first few weeks give the tiny plants extra attention; keep the soil evenly moist and give seedlings sufficient light.

Cuttings

You can snip off the terminal end of a mature small plant and start it in a jar of water and get pretty good results. For

POTTING PLANTS

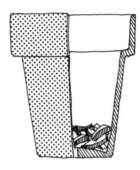

1. Use broken pot particles or small pebbles for drainage material

2. Add mound of soil

3. Center plant on mound and fill with soil

4. Secure plant by packing soil, leaving one inch on top for watering

better results, dip the end of the cutting in rooting hormone powder which you can get at most garden supply outlets, and then place the cutting in a starting medium. To take a stem cutting, snip off about 3 inches of a robust stem; remove the bottom two leaves, but leave on the other leaves. Once the cutting is in place, put a plastic bag over it, and keep the

Small cuttings are being prepared here for their plastic greenhouse bag—a good way to start cuttings. *(Photo courtesy of U.S.D.A.)*

The cuttings (below) will grow at this window until they are ready for separate pots. *(Photo courtesy of U.S.D.A.)*

cutting bed evenly moist and at about 78°F. In a few weeks the new plants—once they have roots—will be ready for individual pots of soil.

To take a leaf cutting, from a plant such as peperomia, remove a leaf, make an X on a leaf with a razor blade, but do *not* cut through the leaf. Now imbed the leaf in a starting medium. When little plants form, pot the cutting separately.

Divisions

You can divide any plant that has clump growth, such as a fern. To determine where the division should be made, look at the plant from above. You'll notice that there are natural divisions, and these are the places to wield the knife. Use a sterile sharp knife, and make the cut directly through the soil and crown of the plant. Separate and crumble away the old soil. Now start the division in fresh soil; keep the soil evenly moist. That's all there is to division.

OTHER PLANT SOURCES

Flea markets usually specialize in furniture, but recently I bought several excellent small plants for practically nothing at a flea market: cacti for two and three dollars, and a rare contorted ivy for two dollars—a species I could never find if I hunted nurseries for years. Just don't be too finicky about how the plant looks at the market. Even if the mature plant is dead, there may be some offsprings that can be salvaged.

Moving companies occasionally have unclaimed furniture—and plant—sales. You can find excellent plant bargains at such sales, but unfortunately these bonanzas are infrequent. Watch your newspaper classified ads for occasional notices of these events.

CHAPTER FIVE

Plants Under Light

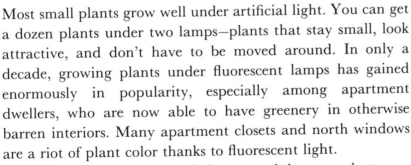

Most small plants grow well under artificial light. You can get a dozen plants under two lamps—plants that stay small, look attractive, and don't have to be moved around. In only a decade, growing plants under fluorescent lamps has gained enormously in popularity, especially among apartment dwellers, who are now able to have greenery in otherwise barren interiors. Many apartment closets and north windows are a riot of plant color thanks to fluorescent light.

There are so many types of plant growth lamps and setups—desk models with canopies, table models, floor models, and so forth—that the selection is bewildering. Many books are devoted specifically to this aspect of gardening, but here's a succinct summary with some special tips and experience-won information. For example, the intensity of the fluorescent light you should give your plants depends on several factors, so here are helpful hints for better fluorescent growing.

1. For germinating seeds and cuttings, use 10 lamp watts per square foot of growing area. For shelf-garden plants like African violets and most foliage plants, use 15 watts per

square foot. For high-energy species like orchids, roses, and other flowering plants, 20 lamp watts of illumination per square foot is beneficial.

2. There is no set rule for how far a plant should be from fluorescent light. Observe your plants; they will tell you when they are getting too much light—leaves will become pale green—or when they are not getting enough light— leaves will be limp.

3. If you add incandescent light to supply the vital infrared rays most conventional fluorescent lamps lack, try the ratio of 4 fluorescent watts to 1 incandescent watt. It's worked well for me. For example, if you have 200 watts of fluorescent light, add 50 watts of incandescent light with five 10-watt bulbs. Do *not* confuse these low light levels of incandescent light with accent lighting, which is different.

4. If the light intensity proves too strong for some plants, move the plants away from the light; set them at the end zones of the lamps, where the light is less intense, or raise the adjustable reflector canopy. On the other hand, if the light

This homemade indoor light setup shows African violets and episcias growing strongly.

is not strong enough for some species, raise them closer to the light source. Put the potted plant on an inverted pot, or use a lattice support.

HOW PLANTS USE LIGHT

Research indicates that plants require blue, red, and far red rays to produce normal growth. The visible spectrum like a rainbow has colors ranging from red to violet. Blue rays enables plants to manufacture carbohydrates, the red controls assimilation of food and also affects the plant's responses to the relative length of light and darkness; far red rays work in conjunction with red in several ways: to control seed germination, stem length in plants, and leaf size by nullifying or reversing the red rays.

Plants grow best when they get sufficient levels of blue and red rays which are in standard fluorescent lamps; incandescent lamps have far red rays. (Some studies claim that the rest of the spectrum is necessary for optimum growth but experiments continue).

FLUORESCENT LAMPS

Fluorescent lamps come in an enormous array of shapes and sizes, with various voltages and wattages and many trade names: cool white, daylight, warm white, natural white, soft white, and, for the lamps designed solely for helping plant growth, Sylvania's "Gro-Lux," Westinghouse's "Plant-Gro," and Durolite's "Vitima." The names for the standard lamps can be misleading because a natural white lamp does not duplicate the sun's light, a daylight lamp does not actually duplicate daylight, and there is no difference to the touch between a cool white and a warm white lamp. Cool white lamps come the closest in providing the red and blue light necessary for plant growth. Daylight lamps are high in blue but low in red light, and warm white and natural white, although high in red light, are deficient in blue wavelengths. Supplemental incandescent light is probably not needed with the special plant lamps because the lamps contain both the red and blue wavelengths.

Newer types of fluorescent lamps have high output (HO) or very high output (VHO) and/or may be grooved (Power Groove from General Electric) or twisted (Powertwist from Durolite). Another development in fluorescent lighting is the square panel manufactured by General Electric. These cool white lamps give the same light as tubular lamps, but they have some advantages: Attractive units can be created with them because the lighting mechanism is concealed, and vertical as well as horizontal lighting is possible. The panel lamp is 12 inches square and only 1-1/2 inches thick. It fits into recessed, surface-mounted, or suspended units and comes in Panel Deluxe, Panel Deluxe Cool, and Cool White in 55 or 80 watts. The Panel Deluxe Cool type brings out vivid color hues, the closest match to natural daylight. Special ballasts are required, and installation of these lamps should be done by an electrician.

LIGHTING

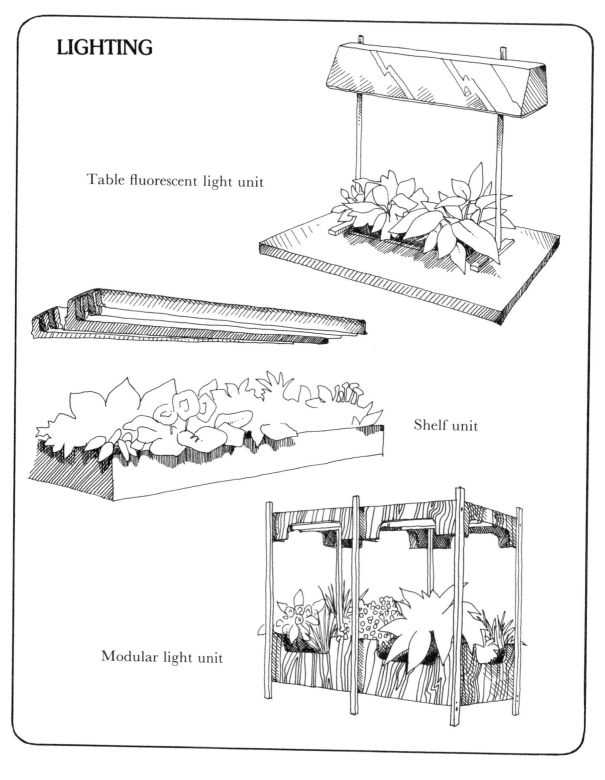

Table fluorescent light unit

Shelf unit

Modular light unit

The Circleline fluorescent lamps have been available for some time, but they are rarely used for plants. They're well designed, give even illumination over a large area, and offer the only practical solution for vertical lighting setups. Somewhat like the old-fashioned fluorescent kitchen fixture, they come in 8- and 10-inch diameters, in 22 or 40 watts. Plant-to-lamp distance should be 26 to 30 inches. Somewhat similar is the new Sylvania Sun Bowl lamp, with a 40-watt bulb, essentially designed for ripening fruit but also an excellent light source for dish garden arrangements.

Remember that no fluorescent lamp can work miracles by itself; plants still need water, humidity, ventilation, and pest control. Some of the lamps may be better than others for plant growth, but plants will grow and prosper under any light if there is enough illumination and sufficient day length. When placing plants under lights, keep in mind that the plants at each end of the lamps grow more slowly than those in the center. And never replace all the lamps at one time; put in one, wait a day, and then put in another to avoid shocking plants with an overabundance of new light.

Start plants rather far away from the lamps, 10 to 12 inches, and gradually raise the plants or lower the lamps after a few weeks; experiment and observe. If the leaves are light green or yellow-green, the plant is getting too much light; raise the lamps. If growth is spindly and stems are elongated, lower the lamps. If you use reading lamps, decreasing the distance from plant to lamp gives twice as much light.

PLANTS FOR FLUORESCENT LIGHT GARDENING

For successful growing, start with plants that need low light intensity. Foliage plants like peperomias, pileas, and bromeliads thrive under lights with little care, and begonias and gesneriads, including the popular African violets, are well-known light-loving plants. As a rule, seedlings and cuttings do better under lamps then they do in natural light. Small succulents and cacti are other good possibilities; I have several dish gardens of them, and they are far superior to the cacti I grow in the garden room. Most miniature and dwarf geraniums can be grown under lights if they are in coolness, and many orchids and bromeliads respond to fluorescent light.

I find it easier to have two medium-sized light gardens than one large one. I group foliage plants, gesneriads, and some begonias in one tray; geraniums, orchids, and bromeliads are in the other growing area. If you're limited to one garden, put the plants that need strong light, such as geraniums, under the center of the lamp, where the light is brightest, and other plants at the ends of the lamps, where light is less intense.

In many of my growing arrangements I keep night temperatures between 52° and 60°F. Of course, like virtually all gardeners, I cannot restrict myself to a certain number of plants. I am forever adding charming ferns, too-tall banana plants, and even carnivorous species, first trying them in one place in the garden, and then moving them about until I find a place where they respond. Plants themselves will, by fresh growth and new buds, tell you if they are happily located. Experimenting is fun, but once a plant starts to respond in one spot, leave it there.

Rosette-type plants grow better under lights than do trailers and hanging plants. Cascading plants in light gardens will

Miniature African violets (top) and dracaenas grow beautifully under lights in this commercial artificial light cart.

eventually become too large for that setting. Then move them to other areas for decoration.

INCANDESCENT LAMPS

Years ago, incandescent lamps were used in small wattages in conjunction with fluorescent lamps. The incandescents furnish far red rays lacking in fluorescent lamps. Today, however, incandescent lamps are used alone, and they do help plants in dim locations. Indeed, you can use an ordinary 60 watt reading lamp as supplemental light for plants but there are also many new plant-growth lamps that fit into standard sockets. You can find them at nurseries and department stores.

There is an advantage in incandescent lighting for plants—they require no special setups or equipment and they look better than the tubular fluorescent lamps which are often limited to use in special units. These units, table or desk models or floor carts come with reflectors and other equipment to accomodate the lamps' tubular design.

Another form of incandescent lighting for plants is what is called accent lighting. Here the light serves a dual purpose: it silhouettes the plants, lending them a dramatic appearance, and it also furnishes needed light for plants in shady places. Called floodlamps, these lights are generally used in can-type fixtures. These fixtures are usually ceiling-mounted and the light is directed at the plants. This is an especially good way to light plants if you have a group in a dim corner or on a table or desk away from natural light. One 150 watt lamp is all that's needed. Always position high wattage floodlamps a reasonable distance (30 to 40 inches) from your plants. Incandescent lamps generate heat which can harm your plants if there's not enough intervening space.

Still another innovation in plant lighting is a lamp that embodies both incandescent and fluorescent rays—both red and blue rays. These lamps fit into standard light sockets. Recent studies show these lamps to be very satisfactory for plant growth; they are inexpensive, easy to use, and a boon to the apartment gardener.

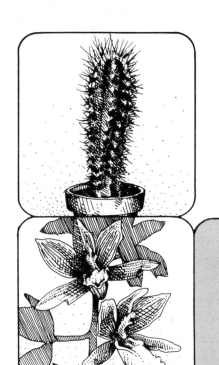

CHAPTER SIX

The Plants

The picture encyclopedia that makes up most of the remainder of this book gives you specific growing recommendations. The chapter you're reading now is a general discussion of the plant groups from which most of those plants come. You may prefer to skip this section, but you'll gain a better understanding of the guidance that's yet to come if you read this carefully.

Botanical names have been used (one must start somewhere); but there are cross-reference listings in the appendix, so you can find the plant by the common name, too. It's wise to get used to botanical names, though; they're actually easy to learn and remember if you pay attention to this explanation.

Each plant family is divided into one or more subfamilies, or clans, each of which is called a genus (the plural is genera). In each genus there are generally several species. For example, philodendron is the genus. In this genus there are many philodendrons, so the species name cordatum makes it specific: that is, Philodendron cordatum. An easy analogy is your name. Your last name corresponds to the genus name, your first name to the species name. Say you are Roger Smith. Smith is the genus (family) name, and Roger is the species (specific) name.

So far that all seems fairly easy, but more is involved. Many nurseries specialize in plant breeding, that is, mating the best with the best to produce a superior plant. These plants have special names following the species name, which simply means that they are improved hybrids: for example, Peperomia caperata 'Golden Ripples.' You can identify such plants by the hybrid name in single quotation marks.

Most indoor gardeners identify plants by common rather than botanical name. For a start this is fine, but it does incur error because common names may differ from one region to another. In some areas Chlorophytum elatum is the spider plant, but in other locales it's called the friendship plant or the airplane plant. So if you are buying or ordering plants by mail, for example, common names are no guarantee you'll get the plant you want. Botanical names (those tongue-twisters you've probably wanted to avoid) are the same worldwide, enabling you to order from any catalogue or purchase plants by name from a knowledgeable source and get exactly what you want.

In the lower shelves of the author's garden room you can see many small plants growing—episcias, marantas—with larger plants on the top shelves.

Sometimes common names refer to all the plants in one plant family. Sansevieria, no matter what its species name, is generally referred to as mother-in-law tongue, or snake plant, although there are many species in the genus.

Small plants make this bathroom attractive. There are bromeliads and miniature orchids to create a colorful habitat. *(Photo by Max Eckert.)*

BROMELIADS

This family of plants includes some species that make excellent indoor subjects because they can tolerate a fair amount of abuse and still survive. Bromeliads have a thick succulent leaf and are shallow-rooted; you needn't give them deep pots. Several bromeliads are vase-shaped; as long as the vase is kept filled with water, the plants will thrive. Keep the potting soil or fir bark just barely moist, never soggy. Bromeliads appreciate good light—the better the light, the better the leaf color. However, even in shade they will survive a long time.

Because of the succulent texture of the leaves, these plants are rarely attacked by insects; that's a definite plus. Most bromeliads have tiny flowers, but it's the bracts that are colorful.

GERANIUMS

Geraniums offer the indoor gardener attractive foliage and colorful flowers for months. Grow these diminutive gems in equal parts of loam and sand. Keep the mix evenly moist (water daily), except in winter, when the plants can be carried somewhat dry. Never let the soil become powdery, though. Geraniums are easy to grow, but they do not tolerate fluctuat-

Geraniums are favorite small indoor plants.

ing temperatures or a stuffy atmosphere. Home temperatures of 65° to 75°F during the day and 55° to 65°F at night suit most kinds of geraniums. Don't be afraid to pinch off the growing tips when the geraniums are young. That will train them to stay small. Give geraniums as much sunshine as possible to promote a good harvest of flowers. Don't fertilize the plants, though, because you want them to stay small.

CACTI AND SUCCULENTS

The Cactus family is huge, with 1,300 species distributed among 200 genera. Most cacti are succulents, but not all succulents are cacti, and the nomenclature of the families can be confusing. Cacti and succulents include some of the most rewarding plants for home culture. They can grow under such adverse conditions as drought and dry atmosphere. A great many in the family are small plants, making them ideal for windowsill growing. Most cacti and succulents are desert plants, but some are from tropical forests. Cacti store water in their thickened stems, which eliminates the need for leaves; succulents, on the other hand, use their fleshy leaves as water reservoirs.

Many of the succulents, especially cacti, must be grown not only dry but cool during their winter rest. Both types of plants

A fine collection of small wall-grown succulents offers a unique way to use plants.

need a sandy soil. I use equal parts of sand and loam. If you want your cacti and succulents to live for years, water them carefully. Although most of these plants prefer to be dry, never let the soil become powdery. In the warm months, most cacti and succulents can take a great deal of water. Grow the plants

Small cacti (above) are excellent for dish gardens. This shows soil, sand, and gravel in the containers to be mixed for making a dish garden.

A collection of small cacti (below) being readied for a dish garden scene.

at a sunny window in winter; the rest of the year they prosper at a west or eastern exposure.

ORCHIDS

Miniature orchids grow lushly in this lovely patio garden room. They are colorful throughout the year.

Miniature orchids are cheerful and colorful. Even though they are not as easy to grow as their larger relatives, they do indeed bloom indoors. Miniature orchids take more time to

adjust to new conditions than most plants: three to five months, depending upon the species. Once established, they come on strong.

For most of the plants you will need 2- or 3-inch pots; slotted clay pots are best. Some miniature orchids have to grow on "rafts" of solidified pieces of osmunda or tree fern. Larger orchids require a definite rest sometime during their growing cycle, but the miniatures generally need moisture all year (there are a few exceptions, which are noted in the descriptions). Do not set potted orchids on a surface; they need bottom ventilation. Place redwood strips 1 inch apart on clay saucers, or put wood strips over pans filled with gravel and place the plants on the strips.

Most miniature orchids grow best in bright light, in a west or east window; only a few need direct sun. The plants, in most cases, will have to be watered daily. Like all orchids, the lilliputian kinds bloom in each of the four seasons.

GESNERIADS

The African violet has been a popular plant for years, but only recently have other gesneriads been accepted as houseplants. In this overlooked group there are some fine indoor subjects, with flowers as pretty, perhaps prettier, than African violets. The lipstick vine, with cascades of scarlet bloom, cannot be ignored, and kohlerias laden with brilliantly colored bell-shaped flowers are stunning at the window. Gloxinias, so easy to grow and so floriferous, are certainly exciting plants. Smithianthias, columneas, and achimenes are a few of the many other gesneriads.

Like orchids, many of the gesneriads come from the tropics, but this does not mean that they must be grown in excessive heat and humidity. Most are comfortable if you are, so average home conditions suit them well.

Some gesneriads—achimenes, kohlerias, smithianthias—have a scaly rhizome at the base of their stem. Others, like rechsteinerias and sinningias, have tuberous roots that act as water storage vessels. Still other gesneriads have fibrous roots.

Most gesneriads need filtered or bright light. Use a loose well-drained soil of equal parts peat moss, leaf mold, garden loam, and sand. Pot the plants carefully; perfect drainage is vital to successful growing. During growth, these plants require plenty of water. Use tepid water because cold water shocks the plants and spots the leaves. Most gesneriads rest after flowering. To rest the plants, place them in a cooler area, say, 50° to 65°F, and keep the soil barely moist. At all times

CARNIVOROUS PLANTS

provide adequate moisture in the air for these plants; 30 to 40 percent humidity will ensure healthy growth.

Not much has been written about these insect-eating plants; most of us are familiar with them only as mammoth, monstrous plants in horror movies. But carnivorous plants bear little resemblance to the movie types. Most plants in the group are small to medium-sized, more bizarre than beautiful. Many are natural bog plants and thus thrive in humidity and shady places. In cultivation, similar conditions are needed. Only a few will grow without glass protection; the majority require the warmth and humidity of a terrarium.

Called cobra plants, Venus fly traps, and pitcher plants, these oddities live on a diet of insects attracted to the plant's odor. Once ensnared, the insect is digested by the plant by means of internal chemical fluids. The digested nutrients are absorbed by the plant tissue. If your home is not an insect haven, don't fret that the plants will starve: A tiny grain of hamburger fed by hand once a month does the job.

If you want to keep your carnivorous plants for some time, grow them in a terrarium. Use a planting bed of equal parts crushed charcoal and tiny stone. Spread a 2- to 3-inch blanket

The popular Venus fly trap is a miniature plant that offers hours of fascination. *(Photo courtesy of Burpee Seed Co.)*

of sphagnum moss. Sink the pots to their rims in the medium, or take the plants out of their containers and pot them in the bedding. Keep the terrarium out of sun but in bright light. Water the plants moderately; the "soil" should always be slightly damp. To increase the humidity, cover the terrarium with a pane of glass, and lift it occasionally to allow air to circulate inside.

BULBS

It takes very little effort to make bulbs bloom indoors for spring color. Even a novice gardener can be assured of a display at the window if the bulbs are planted in late fall. Tulips, daffodils, crocuses, hyacinths, and scilla are forcing bulbs, which means that they can be made to bloom indoors ahead of their natural outdoor schedule. Purchase firm healthy bulbs from reputable dealers; do not look for bargains. Plant the bulbs from October to February, in a soil mixture of equal parts of humus, sand, and peat moss. Stagger the potting schedule so you'll have color over a long period. For example, plant tulip, daffodil, or hyacinth bulbs in mid-December for late January bloom, in late January for early March bloom, and in early February for late March flowers.

A 5-inch pot accommodates one daffodil or one hyacinth. An 8-inch bulb pan, a shallow pot, is ideal for several tulips. Plant forcing bulbs so the necks of the bulbs rest slightly above the soil line. After potting the bulbs, moisten the soil well. Now arrange for a period of rooting. Place the pots in a pan or box (a fruit crate is good), and pack moist peat moss between and over the pots, filling the box. Put the bulbs in 40- to 50-degree temperature in a dark spot, and keep the potting mix evenly moist, never soggy and never too dry.

When pots are filled with roots (six to nine weeks, depending on the type of bulb planted), remove the pots from the box and bring them into light. They are now ready for forcing. The time required to produce bloom varies according to temperature, light, varieties being grown, and time of year. Forcing early in the season at 62 to 72 degrees takes about four weeks until bloom. The colder the temperature, the slower the blooms develop. When top growth shows, move the plants to a sunny window and keep the soil just moist.

Flowers last for about two weeks if they are grown with even moisture and in coolness (70°F). If you want to keep your hardy bulbs after they flower, water them until the leaves wither naturally; then plant them in the garden. If left outdoors, the bulbs can be used again the following season, although the bloom may not be plentiful. If you do not have a garden, discard the bulbs; it is useless to try to force them again indoors.

Tender spring-flowering bulbs that need no cold, shade, and out-of-season forcing to make them bloom can be started when you get them. These bulbs include paperwhite narcissus, French Roman hyacinths, colchicum, and amaryllis. Narcissus, hyacinth, and colchicum can be grown in plain water or in water and pebbles. Pot amaryllis in the same mixture used for forced bulbs.

FERNS

The ferns, as a group, offer a dazzling array of foliage accent. There are ferns with lacy fronds, others have wild bold fronds, some are delicate, and many are fragile in appearance. In nature, ferns grow in moist, cool, and shady locations.

Place ferns in filtered light, and give them a very porous soil of equal parts loam, leaf mold, and sand. Keep them moist but never soggy. I do not feed ferns because fertilizer often burns the leaf tips; the plants grow better without additional feeding.

Ferns should rest in winter, so decrease the moisture and keep the soil barely moist. Grow plants in small pots, and disturb them as seldom as possible. If you can, put the pots on pebbles in trays so that adequate moisture is provided: 50 percent humidity is ideal.

BEGONIAS

The Begonia family offers hundreds of fine small plants for indoor growing; at one time I grew sixty of these diminuitive gems. The plants are varied: some are valued for their colorful foliage (the rex group, for example), and others like the angel-wings have colorful flowers. You can use small begonias in so many ways, too: In terrariums and dish gardens, under lights, or simply as decoration for tables and desks.

Most begonias are easy to grow; they need a porous soil that drains readily and bright light. Keep them in a place where there is a good circulation of air and where humidity is between 20 and 50 percent. (Watering suggestions for plants are in the plant encyclopedia) and average home temperatures suit most begonias.

In summer, begonias do not tolerate direct sun so shade them with a curtain at the window; the rest of the year, however, they do appreciate bright light and some sun.

Try not to get water on the leaves of plants and if you mist the growing area, be sure it is in the early morning so plants can dry out before night. Too much moisture and low night temperatures can cause disease.

As mentioned, begonias do very well as terrarium subjects and are equally attractive in dish gardens. These are favorite

Here, some small rex begonias grow under a dome—an ideal home for moisture-loving plants.

Small begonias such as this one also make a pretty spot of color and are easy to grow.

plants of many gardeners and after you grow some you will see why. They are perhaps the most colorful leaf plant of the many indoor plants we have.

ROSES

There is an incredible array of miniature roses, cousins to the larger garden types, and these diminutive beauties create a sensation at windows. Most of the small roses grow only 4 inches and bear a harvest of flowers. All that beauty is not easy to achieve, however. Tiny roses require care; they must be trimmed and clipped occasionally, and leaves must be washed. Perhaps most important, roses really do need cool temperatures (60°F) to thrive. I was most successful when I grew my miniature roses in an unheated pantry in Chicago where temperatures were 55° to 65°F during winter and about 5 degrees higher during the day.

If you have a cool place, miniature roses will grow and bloom year after year. They require a porous soil and copious amounts of water during spring and summer. Keep them evenly moist the rest of the year and guard them against insect attack. It seems that red spiders consider roses a gourmet delight, so be prepared. (See Chapter 2.) Also be sure that the growing area has good ventilation; roses hate a stagnant atmosphere.

For all their idiosyncrasies, miniature roses are definitely worth growing. There are hundreds of them coming in a myriad of colors—orange and red are my favorites, but white and pink may be yours. Do try some.

OTHER PLANT GROUPS

It would be impossible in a book of this size to cover every plant group that includes many small plants. But I did want to mention those families which include more miniatures than do other families, and these include Peperomias and Pileas. There are a great many tiny plants in these groups, and they are ideal houseplants able to withstand neglect if necessary and still thrive.

Peperomias have small rounded leaves, usually glossy green and succulent in texture. Generally, they like a great deal of water and do best with ample moisture, but some can get along with less. Sun is not necessary to bring these plants to perfection. They grow beautifully in bright light. You'll find over a dozen different kinds listed in the next chapter.

Pileas are also handsome plants, and many are small-leaved and small in habit. They need somewhat more care than, say, peperomias but are usually quite worthwhile. Keep the plants in a bright place and the soil evenly moist. Some pileas have variegated leaves which are somewhat textured; do not get water on them. Other pileas are smooth-textured and plain green.

You will also find some wildflowers in the encyclopedia section; these are difficult to raise as pot plants, but they are worth the challenge and some do eventually adjust to indoor conditions.

Echeverias in small bonsai pots make a handsome statement at this window.

A small orange tree makes a handsome picture. They can be grown indoors or out. *(Photo courtesy of California Redwood Association.)*

CHAPTER SEVEN

The Plant Picture Encyclopedia

The following pages cover 500 small plants of various kinds. Some are easy to grow, some are difficult, but none are impossible. Proper care instructions and descriptions are given for each plant along with an identification drawing to help you select plants you'll like.

Insofar as was possible, *Hortus III* (prepared by the staff of the L. H. Bailey Hortorium) was used for botanical nomenclature. *Exotica 6* by A. F. Graf was also used. In some cases, I opted to use a more common spelling than the botanical one, conforming to the usual usage in plant suppliers' catalogues.

The plants were drawn from specimens in my collection, from friend's collections, and of course from plants in several greenhouses, notably Golden Gate Conservatory and the Berkeley Botanical Garden greenhouses.

ACHIMENES 'CHARM'

DESCRIPTION: Compact with dark green leaves, pink flowers.

REMARKS: Start from corms; good color for summer.

SIZE: To 12 inches

TEMPERATURE: 72°–80°F

HUMIDITY: 30 percent

WATERING: Keep evenly moist

LIGHT: Sun

ACHIMENES 'MINIATA'

DESCRIPTION: Trailing habit; small oval green leaves, large purplish-red flowers.

REMARKS: Start from corms: good color for summer.

SIZE: To 14 inches

TEMPERATURE: 72°–80°F

HUMIDITY: 30 percent

WATERING: Keep evenly moist

LIGHT: Sun

ACHIMENES MISERA

DESCRIPTION: Toothed gray-green leaves, lilac flowers.

REMARKS: Start from corms; good color for summer.

SIZE: To 14 inches

TEMPERATURE: 72°–80°F

HUMIDITY: 30 percent

WATERING: Keep evenly moist

LIGHT: Sun

ACIDANTHERA BICOLOR

DESCRIPTION: Grassy leaves and charming white flowers with a spot of purple.

REMARKS: After flowering, rest bulbs in pots in shady place. Apply scant watering.

SIZE: To 20 inches

TEMPERATURE: 58°–65°F

HUMIDITY: 30 percent

WATERING: Keep evenly moist

LIGHT: Bright light

ACORUS GRAMINEUS (flagplant)

DESCRIPTION: Handsome tiny foliage plant with grassy leaves; grows to 10 inches.

REMARKS: Fine grassy plant; decorative and easy to grow.

SIZE: To 10 inches

TEMPERATURE: 65°–75°F

HUMIDITY: 30 percent

WATERING: Keep very wet

LIGHT: Shade or bright

ADIANTUM CUNEATUM GRACILLIMUM (maidenhair fern)

DESCRIPTION: Small fern with very lacy emerald green fronds.

SIZE: To 20 inches

TEMPERATURE: 70°–78°F

HUMIDITY: 30 percent

WATERING: Keep evenly moist

REMARKS: Pot in equal parts fir bark and soil.

LIGHT: Bright

ADIANTUM PEDATUM

DESCRIPTION: Graceful curved fronds, emerald green. Handsome.

SIZE: To 20 inches

TEMPERATURE: 70°–78°F

HUMIDITY: 30 percent

WATERING: Keep evenly moist

REMARKS: Nice, graceful; pot in equal parts fir bark and soil.

LIGHT: Bright

ADROMISCHUS CLAVIFOLIUS

DESCRIPTION: Clusters of fat club-shaped silver-green leaves.

SIZE: To 3 inches

TEMPERATURE: 70°–80°F

HUMIDITY: 30 percent

WATERING: Dry out between waterings

REMARKS: Fine succulent, easy to grow.

LIGHT: Bright

ADROMISCHUS COOPERI (plover eggs)

DESCRIPTION: Small club-shaped leaves dotted with red.

SIZE: To 6 inches

TEMPERATURE: 70–80°F

HUMIDITY: 30 percent

WATERING: Dry out between waterings

REMARKS: Handsome succulent, easy to grow.

LIGHT: Bright

ADROMISCHUS MACULATUS (calico hearts)

DESCRIPTION: Thick, chocolate brown foliage; sculptural.

SIZE: To 10 inches

TEMPERATURE: 70°–80°F

HUMIDITY: 30 percent

WATERING: Dry out between waterings

REMARKS: Another good small succulent; ideal for dish gardens.

LIGHT: Bright

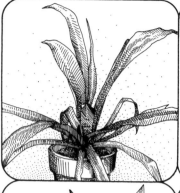

AECHMEA FILICAULIS

DESCRIPTION: Leaves are glossy green; white flowers.

SIZE: To 18 inches

TEMPERATURE: 70°–78°F

HUMIDITY: 30 percent

WATERING: Keep evenly moist

REMARKS: Vase-shaped decorative plant; easy to grow.

LIGHT: Sun

AECHMEA MERTENSII

DESCRIPTION: Green leaves, red and yellow flowers.

SIZE: To 14 inches

TEMPERATURE: 70°–78°F

HUMIDITY: 30 percent

WATERING: Keep evenly moist

REMARKS: Not spectacular but easy to grow.

LIGHT: Sun

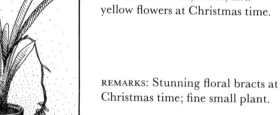

AECHMEA RACINAE

DESCRIPTION: Red, black, and yellow flowers at Christmas time.

SIZE: To 10 inches

TEMPERATURE: 70°–80°F

HUMIDITY: 30 percent

WATERING: Keep evenly moist

REMARKS: Stunning floral bracts at Christmas time; fine small plant.

LIGHT: Sun

AECHMEA RECURVATA

DESCRIPTION: Vase-shaped; dark green leaves, pink flowers.

SIZE: To 20 inches

TEMPERATURE: 70°–80°F

HUMIDITY: 30 percent

WATERING: Keep evenly moist

REMARKS: Handsome variegated leaves; vase-shaped and easy to grow.

LIGHT: Sun

AEONIUM ATROPURPUREUM

DESCRIPTION: Coppery-red leaves; golden yellow flowers.

SIZE: To 12 inches

TEMPERATURE: 70°–80°F

HUMIDITY: 30 percent

WATERING: Keep evenly moist

REMARKS: Unusual pot plant; use as table decoration.

LIGHT: Bright

AEONIUM CANARIENSE

DESCRIPTION: Large flattened rosette of apple green leaves.

REMARKS: Unusual succulent; grows by itself.

SIZE: To 10 inches

TEMPERATURE: 70°–78°F

HUMIDITY: 30 percent

WATERING: Keep evenly moist

LIGHT: Bright

AERIDES CRASSIFOLIUM

DESCRIPTION: Amethyst purple blooms, generally spotted.

REMARKS: Dependable small orchid; mist frequently.

SIZE: To 10 inches

TEMPERATURE: 70°–80°F

HUMIDITY: 30 percent

WATERING: Dry out between waterings

LIGHT: Sun

AERIDES JAPONICUM

DESCRIPTION: Greenish-white flowers marked with purple ridges. Fragrant.

REMARKS: Another dependable orchid.

SIZE: To 10 inches

TEMPERATURE: 70°–80°F

HUMIDITY: 30 percent

WATERING: Dry out between waterings

LIGHT: Sun

AGAVE FILIFERA

DESCRIPTION: Narrow olive green leaves with loose curled threads at margins.

REMARKS: No flowers but a dependable succulent plant.

SIZE: To 10 inches

TEMPERATURE: 70°–78°F

HUMIDITY: 30 percent

WATERING: Dry out between waterings

LIGHT: Bright

AGAVE PICTA

DESCRIPTION: Narrow pale green leaves with white margins, small black teeth.

REMARKS: Grows well indoors; good for dish gardens.

SIZE: To 10 inches

TEMPERATURE: 70°–78°F

HUMIDITY: 30 percent

WATERING: Dry out between waterings

LIGHT: Bright

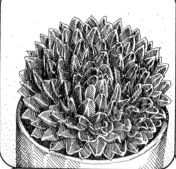

AGAVE VICTORAE REGINAE

DESCRIPTION: Olive green leaves penciled with white edges.

SIZE: To 12 inches

TEMPERATURE: 70°–78°F

HUMIDITY: 30 percent

REMARKS: Spectacular plant; beautiful symmetry and easy to grow.

WATERING: Dry out between waterings

LIGHT: Bright

AGLAONEMA COMMUTATUM (Chinese evergreen)

DESCRIPTION: Branching growth; lance-shaped green leaves marked with silver.

SIZE: To 16 inches

TEMPERATURE: 70°–78°F

HUMIDITY: 20–30 percent

REMARKS: Potbound plants will bloom in late summer.

WATERING: Dry out between waterings

LIGHT: Bright

AGLAONEMA PICTUM

DESCRIPTION: Dark green leaves with silver spots; branching growth.

SIZE: To 12 inches

TEMPERATURE: 70°–78°F

HUMIDITY: 20–30 percent

REMARKS: Can be grown in vase of water.

WATERING: Dry out between waterings

LIGHT: Bright

ALLOPHYTUM MEXICANUM (Mexican foxglove)

DESCRIPTION: Long dark green leathery leaves; tubular lavendar flowers.

SIZE: To 10 inches

TEMPERATURE: 55°–70°F

HUMIDITY: 40 percent

REMARKS: Charming decorative plant for table or desk.

WATERING: Keep evenly moist

LIGHT: Sun

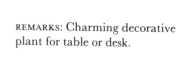

ALOE ARISTATA (lace aloe)

DESCRIPTION: Green-gray rosette dotted white and tipped with white marginal teeth.

SIZE: To 6 inches

TEMPERATURE: 60°–75°F

HUMIDITY: 20–40 percent

REMARKS: Use a well-drained potting medium of equal parts sand and soil.

WATERING: Dry out between waterings

LIGHT: Sun

ALOE BREVIFOLIA

DESCRIPTION: Gray-green rosette; bears tall spike of red flowers.

SIZE: To 4 inches

TEMPERATURE: 60°–75°F

HUMIDITY: 20–40 percent

WATERING: Dry out between waterings

LIGHT: Sun

REMARKS: Nice dish garden plant. Easy to grow.

ALOE CILIARIS

DESCRIPTION: Toothed green-white leaves with spiraling growth and pencil stems.

SIZE: To 6 inches

TEMPERATURE: 60°–75°F

HUMIDITY: 20–40 percent

WATERING: Dry out between waterings

LIGHT: Sun

REMARKS: Another handsome succulent for desk or table decoration.

ALOE NOBILIS (gold-striped aloe)

DESCRIPTION: Bright green leaves edged yellow.

SIZE: To 20 inches

TEMPERATURE: 60°–75°F

HUMIDITY: 20–40 percent

WATERING: Dry out between waterings

LIGHT: Sun

REMARKS: Somewhat large but handsome and worth the space.

ALOE STRIATA

DESCRIPTION: Stiff pointed gray-green leaves with narrow pinkish edge.

SIZE: To 12 inches

TEMPERATURE: 60°–75°F

HUMIDITY: 20–40 percent

WATERING: Dry out between waterings

LIGHT: Sun

REMARKS: Handsome aloe; good for dish gardens, table decoration.

ALOE VARIEGATA (partridge-breast aloe)

DESCRIPTION: Waxy bands of white markings on green leaves.

SIZE: To 12 inches

TEMPERATURE: 60°–75°F

HUMIDITY: 20–40 percent

WATERING: Dry out between waterings

LIGHT: Sun

REMARKS: Handsome white and green leaves make this one very desirable.

ALTERNANTHERA BETTZICKIANA

DESCRIPTION: Clustering herb with narrow twisted leaves, creamy yellow to salmon red.

SIZE: To 12 inches

TEMPERATURE: 70°–80°F

HUMIDITY: 20–40 percent

WATERING: Keep on dry side

REMARKS: Great window plant with decorative leaves; unusual.

LIGHT: Sun

ALTERNANTHERA VERSICOLOR

DESCRIPTION: Broad almost round dark green leaves with purplish-carmine veining edged pink.

SIZE: To 3 inches

TEMPERATURE: 70°–80°F

HUMIDITY: 20–40 percent

WATERING: Keep on dry side

REMARKS: Unique, worth the search; okay for basket growing.

LIGHT: Sun

ANGRAECUM FALCATUM

DESCRIPTION: Straplike leathery leaves and white flowers with long spurs.

SIZE: To 6 inches

TEMPERATURE: 55°–70°F

HUMIDITY: 40 percent

WATERING: Keep evenly moist

REMARKS: More difficult to grow than most orchids but worth the try.

LIGHT: Sun

ANTHURIUM SCHERZERIANUM

DESCRIPTION: Green leaves on tall stems and brilliant red waxy flowers.

SIZE: To 14 inches

TEMPERATURE: 65°–78°F

REMARKS: Floral spathes stay red for months; somewhat temperamental plant; keep out of drafts.

HUMIDITY: 60 percent

WATERING: Keep very moist

LIGHT: Sun

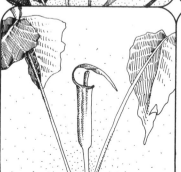

ARISAEMA TRIPHYLLUM (jack-in-the-pulpit)

DESCRIPTION: Dark green leaves and funnel-shaped odd flowers.

SIZE: To 14 inches

TEMPERATURE: 60°–70°F

HUMIDITY: 50 percent

WATERING: Keep quite moist

REMARKS: Tough one to grow indoors but succeeds in terrarium.

LIGHT: Shade

ASCOCENTRUM MINIATUM

DESCRIPTION: Small orchid with short erect stem and leathery leaves; pendant stem of small red-orange flowers.

REMARKS: Don't miss this one; has bright orange flowers in summer.

SIZE: To 10 inches

TEMPERATURE: 72°–80°F

HUMIDITY: 50 percent

WATERING: Keep evenly moist

LIGHT: Sun

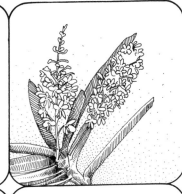

ASPLENIUM PLATYNEURON (spleenwort)

DESCRIPTION: Feathery fronds and brown-purple stems.

REMARKS: Grow in equal parts fir bark and soil for best results. Repot yearly.

SIZE: To 16 inches

TEMPERATURE: 55°–75°F

HUMIDITY: 40 percent

WATERING: Keep quite moist

LIGHT: Shade

ASPLENIUM TRICHOMANES (maidenhair spleenwort)

DESCRIPTION: Clustered fronds and 1-inch leaflets on black stems.

REMARKS: Graceful and handsome; repot yearly.

SIZE: To 18 inches

TEMPERATURE: 55°–75°F

HUMIDITY: 40 percent

WATERING: Keep quite moist

LIGHT: Shade

AZALEA 'GUMPO'

DESCRIPTION: Bushy plant with dark green leaves and brilliant red flowers.

REMARKS: One of the few azaleas that will respond indoors.

SIZE: To 10 inches

TEMPERATURE: 55°–70°F

HUMIDITY: 40 percent

WATERING: Keep quite moist

LIGHT: Bright

BAMBUSA NANA (miniature bamboo)

DESCRIPTION: Thin stems with feathery apple green leaves.

REMARKS: Likes buckets of water and an airy place; grows like a weed.

SIZE: To 20 inches

TEMPERATURE: 60°–78°F

HUMIDITY: 40 percent

WATERING: Keep very wet

LIGHT: Bright

BEGONIA 'ALBO PICTA'

DESCRIPTION: Narrow silver-spotted leaves and whitish-pink blooms

REMARKS: Handsome and good in hanging basket; give some winter sun.

SIZE: To 20 inches

TEMPERATURE: 75°–80°F

HUMIDITY: 30 percent

WATERING: Keep evenly moist

LIGHT: Bright

BEGONIA ARIDICAULIS

DESCRIPTION: Light green leaves sharply tapered; flower white in late winter.

REMARKS: Good species begonia; unusual and adapts to indoor culture.

SIZE: To 14 inches

TEMPERATURE: 75°–80°F

HUMIDITY: 30 percent

WATERING: Keep evenly moist

LIGHT: Bright

BEGONIA BOWERI (eyelash begonia)

DESCRIPTION: Green leaves stitched with black at edges; bushy growth.

REMARKS: Stunning plant; worth space in any indoor garden.

SIZE: To 12 inches

TEMPERATURE: 70°–80°F

HUMIDITY: 30 percent

WATERING: Keep evenly moist

LIGHT: Bright

BEGONIA 'BOW CHANCE'

DESCRIPTION: Yellow and green leaves; bushy growth.

REMARKS: One of the outstanding hybrids; excellent for table or desk accent.

SIZE: To 12 inches

TEMPERATURE: 75°–80 F

HUMIDITY: 30 percent

WATERING: Keep evenly moist

LIGHT: Bright

BEGONIA 'BOW NIGRA'

DESCRIPTION: Star-shaped, bronzy leaves light green in center and along veins; blush pink flowers.

REMARKS: Great leaf color; somewhat temperamental. Likes good air circulation.

SIZE: To 14 inches

TEMPERATURE: 75°–80°F

HUMIDITY: 30 percent

WATERING: Keep evenly moist

LIGHT: Bright

89

BEGONIA 'CALICO'

DESCRIPTION: Rounded silver-dotted leaves flushed red.

REMARKS: Pretty as a picture and easy to grow.

SIZE: To 10 inches

TEMPERATURE: 75°–80°F

HUMIDITY: 30 percent

WATERING: Keep evenly moist

LIGHT: Bright

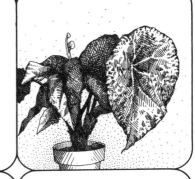

BEGONIA 'CHANTILLY LACE'

DESCRIPTION: Chartreuse leaves with black stitches around edge; clusters of pink flowers in winter.

REMARKS: Exquisite leaves; keep in airy place.

SIZE: To 14 inches

TEMPERATURE: 75°–80°F

HUMIDITY: 30 percent

WATERING: Keep evenly moist

LIGHT: Bright

BEGONIA 'CHINA DOLL'

DESCRIPTION: Light green to purple leaves, pink blooms.

REMARKS: Always popular and easy to grow indoors.

SIZE: To 8 inches

TEMPERATURE: 75°–80°F

HUMIDITY: 30 percent

WATERING: Keep evenly moist

LIGHT: Bright

BEGONIA 'DEW DROP'

DESCRIPTION: Rainbow hues; tiny leaves and bushy growth.

REMARKS: Delightful small begonia.

SIZE: To 6 inches

TEMPERATURE: 75°–80°F

HUMIDITY: 30 percent

WATERING: Keep evenly moist

LIGHT: Bright

BEGONIA DREGEI (maple-leaf begonia)

DESCRIPTION: Bronze-green thin leaves with purple veins; flowers white.

REMARKS: Grown for its unusual leaves; nice branching plant that makes good room accent.

SIZE: To 14 inches

TEMPERATURE: 70°–80°F

HUMIDITY: 30 percent

WATERING: Keep somewhat dry

LIGHT: Bright

BEGONIA FOLIOSA (fern begonia)

DESCRIPTION: Tiny, waxy, bronze-green oval leaves notched toward tip; tiny blush-white flower.

REMARKS: Can be grown in a basket; very pretty and hardy; leaves like a fern.

SIZE: To 16 inches

TEMPERATURE: 70°–80°F

HUMIDITY: 20–40 percent

WATERING: Keep somewhat moist

LIGHT: Shade

BEGONIA GRIFFITHI

DESCRIPTION: Heart-shaped downy leaves, ruby and emerald with rose bands and white flowers.

REMARKS: A real exotic that needs some pampering.

SIZE: To 14 inches

TEMPERATURE: 72°–85°F

HUMIDITY: 60 percent

WATERING: Keep evenly moist

LIGHT: Shade

BEGONIA HYDROCOTYLIFOLIA (pennywort begonia)

DESCRIPTION: Rounded, thick waxy leaves, light olive green with dark veins; small rosy flowers.

REMARKS: A fine rhizmatous begonia that does well even with little care.

SIZE: To 10 inches

TEMPERATURE: 72°–80°F

HUMIDITY: 30 percent

WATERING: Dry out between waterings

LIGHT: Bright

BEGONIA 'IVY EVER'

DESCRIPTION: Glossy green leaves, pink flowers.

REMARKS: Good basket plant; grows fast.

SIZE: To 20 inches

TEMPERATURE: 72°–80°F

HUMIDITY: 30 percent

WATERING: Dry out between waterings

LIGHT: Bright

BEGONIA 'LUCILLE CLOSSON'

DESCRIPTION: Almost black leaves with irregular markings, pink flowers.

REMARKS: One of the best hybrids; robust and easy to grow.

SIZE: To 20 inches

TEMPERATURE: 72°–80°F

HUMIDITY: 30 percent

WATERING: Dry out between waterings

LIGHT: Bright

BEGONIA 'LULANDI'

DESCRIPTION: Evergreen spreading plant with bright green long pointed broad leaves; large pink flowers.

REMARKS: Good upright growing begonia.

SIZE: To 16 inches

TEMPERATURE: 70°–80°F

HUMIDITY: 30 percent

WATERING: Dry out between waterings

LIGHT: Bright

BEGONIA MEDORA

DESCRIPTION: Glossy green silver-spotted leaves, large pink flowers.

REMARKS: Exquisite foliage; keep out of drafts.

SIZE: To 14 inches

TEMPERATURE: 75°–85°F

HUMIDITY: 30 percent

WATERING: Dry out between waterings

LIGHT: Bright

BEGONIA 'ORANGE DAINTY'

DESCRIPTION: Small lustrous dark green leaves; pendant clusters of orange flowers.

REMARKS: Charming; give some sun in winter. Flowers on and off throughout the year.

SIZE: To 14 inches

TEMPERATURE: 72°–80°F

HUMIDITY: 30 percent

WATERING: Keep evenly moist

LIGHT: Bright

BEGONIA 'PANSY'

DESCRIPTION: Pointed green leaves and metallic green overlay.

REMARKS: Nice accent but somewhat difficult to grow.

SIZE: To 10 inches

TEMPERATURE: 72°–80°F

HUMIDITY: 30 percent

WATERING: Keep evenly moist

LIGHT: Bright

BEGONIA 'PERIDOT'

DESCRIPTION: Tiny button-like leaves, dark red, silver spotted.

REMARKS: Always good; robust and popular.

SIZE: To 8 inches

TEMPERATURE: 72°–80°F

HUMIDITY: 30 percent

WATERING: Keep evenly moist

LIGHT: Bright

BEGONIA 'RED BERRY'

DESCRIPTION: Wine red foliage; branching.

REMARKS: A very fine rex type begonia; sometimes dies down in winter.

SIZE: To 10 inches

TEMPERATURE: 72°–80°F

HUMIDITY: 50 percent

WATERING: Keep evenly moist

LIGHT: Shade

BEGONIA 'RED WING'

DESCRIPTION: Silver edges, wine red leaves.

REMARKS: Sometimes dies down in winter; Rex type.

SIZE: To 10 inches

TEMPERATURE: 72°–80°F

HUMIDITY: 50 percent

WATERING: Keep evenly moist

LIGHT: Shade

BEGONIA RICHARDSIANA

DESCRIPTION: Light green leaves, lobed with a red spot at the juncture of the long lobes; white flowers.

REMARKS: Good one for the beginner.

SIZE: To 14 inches

TEMPERATURE: 72°–78°F

HUMIDITY: 20–40 percent

WATERING: Keep evenly moist

LIGHT: Bright

BEGONIA 'ROSA KUGEL'

DESCRIPTION: Small green leaves, pink flowers.

REMARKS: A favorite and grows fast. Excellent for indoor decoration.

SIZE: To 8 inches

TEMPERATURE: 72°–78°F

HUMIDITY: 20–40 percent

WATERING: Keep evenly moist

LIGHT: Bright

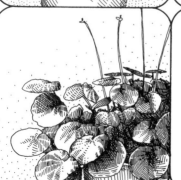

BEGONIA ROTUNDIFOLIA

DESCRIPTION: Light green round leaves, pink flowers.

REMARKS: Another satisfactory begonia.

SIZE: To 12 inches

TEMPERATURE: 72°–78°F

HUMIDITY: 20–40 percent

WATERING: Keep evenly moist

LIGHT: Bright

BEGONIA 'SPAULDING'

DESCRIPTION: Rounded leaves, beautiful grass green color.

REMARKS: Good hybrid, robust and grows easily.

SIZE: To 8 inches

TEMPERATURE: 72°–78°F

HUMIDITY: 20–40 percent

WATERING: Keep evenly moist

LIGHT: Bright

BEGONIA 'VIRBOB'

DESCRIPTION: Small star-shaped leaf richly marked green, chartreuse, bronze, and deep red.

REMARKS: Nice in hanging basket; keep out of drafts.

SIZE: To 14 inches

TEMPERATURE: 72°–78°F

HUMIDITY: 20–40 percent

WATERING: Keep evenly moist

LIGHT: Bright

BEGONIA WELTONIENSIS

DESCRIPTION: Somewhat large green leaves, pink flowers.

REMARKS: Slow growing but does well indoors.

SIZE: To 12 inches

TEMPERATURE: 72°–78°F

HUMIDITY: 20–40 percent

WATERING: Keep evenly moist

LIGHT: Bright

BEGONIA 'WINTER QUEEN'

DESCRIPTION: Frosty green leaves dusted with silver; dainty white flowers in winter.

REMARKS: Difficult to grow but worth the try.

SIZE: To 10 inches

TEMPERATURE: 72°–78°F

HUMIDITY: 20–40 percent

WATERING: Keep evenly moist

LIGHT: Bright

BEGONIA 'WOOD NYMPH'

DESCRIPTION: Thrush brown leaves overlaid with silver.

REMARKS: Delightful imp with exquisite flowers. Needs some winter sun.

SIZE: To 8 inches

TEMPERATURE: 72°–78°F

HUMIDITY: 20–40 percent

WATERING: Keep evenly moist

LIGHT: Bright

BERTOLONIA MACULATA

DESCRIPTION: Hairy, dark green leaves shaded bright moss green along center, deep red beneath.

SIZE: To 12 inches

TEMPERATURE: 75°–85°F

HUMIDITY: 40 percent

WATERING: Dry out between waterings

LIGHT: Bright

REMARKS: Different and worth a spot in the indoor garden.

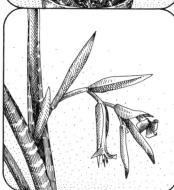

BILLBERGIA DISTACHIA

DESCRIPTION: Pinkish-brown leaves, green and blue flowers.

SIZE: To 14 inches

TEMPERATURE: 70°–80°F

HUMIDITY: 20–40 percent

WATERING: Keep evenly moist

LIGHT: Sun

REMARKS: Undemanding bromeliad; vase-shaped and grows well indoors.

BILLBERGIA EUPHEMIAE

DESCRIPTION: Leaves gray-green; flowers pink, blue.

SIZE: To 16 inches

TEMPERATURE: 70°–80°F

HUMIDITY: 20–40 percent

WATERING: Keep evenly moist

LIGHT: Sun

REMARKS: Good window plant.

BILLBERGIA LEPTOPODA

DESCRIPTION: Leaves green, spotted cream color; flowers green and blue.

SIZE: To 14 inches

TEMPERATURE: 70°–80°F

HUMIDITY: 20–40 percent

WATERING: Keep evenly moist

LIGHT: Sun

REMARKS: Grow in equal parts fir bark and soil; easy to grow.

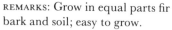

BILLBERGIA NUTANS (queen's tears)

DESCRIPTION: Leaves green; flower cerise. Vase-shaped plant.

SIZE: To 10 inches

TEMPERATURE: 70°–80°F

HUMIDITY: 20–40 percent

WATERING: Keep evenly moist

LIGHT: Sun

REMARKS: Grow in equal parts fir bark and soil; easy to grow.

BRASSAVOLA CUCULLATA

DESCRIPTION: Orchid with stemlike pseudobulbs and solitary leaf; white flowers.

REMARKS: Needs plenty of sun; difficult orchid to bloom but worth the effort.

SIZE: To 8 inches

TEMPERATURE: 55°–70°F

HUMIDITY: 40 percent

WATERING: Keep somewhat dry

LIGHT: Sun

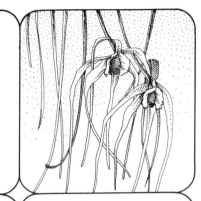

BRASSAVOLA GLAUCA

DESCRIPTION: Small bluish-gray orchid with slender pseudobulbs bearing a stiff glaucous leaf; fragrant white flowers.

REMARKS: The handsome scented flowers last a long time.

SIZE: To 12 inches

TEMPERATURE: 55°–70°F

HUMIDITY: 40 percent

WATERING: Keep somewhat dry

LIGHT: Sun

BRASSAVOLA NODOSA (lady-of-the-night)

DESCRIPTION: Orchid with stemlike pseudobulbs and a solitary stout leaf; white flowers.

REMARKS: An absolute stellar orchid; takes time to adjust to indoor conditions; grow on cork.

SIZE: To 8 inches

TEMPERATURE: 55°–70°F

HUMIDITY: 40 percent

WATERING: Keep somewhat dry

LIGHT: Sun

BROUGHTONIA SANGUINEA

DESCRIPTION: Small orchid with flat green leaves; flowers crimson-scarlet.

REMARKS: Flowers on and off throughout the year; easy to grow.

SIZE: To 10 inches

TEMPERATURE: 55°–70°F

HUMIDITY: 40 percent

WATERING: Keep somewhat dry

LIGHT: Sun

BULBOPHYLLUM BARBIGERUM

DESCRIPTION: Orchid with flattened pseudobulbs bearing solitary leaf 3 inches long; flowers greenish-brown with yellow markings.

REMARKS: Grows best in tree fern slab; mist with water frequently.

SIZE: To 2 inches

TEMPERATURE: 72°–85°F

HUMIDITY: 50 percent

WATERING: Keep evenly moist

LIGHT: Sun

BULBOPHYLLUM LEOPARDINUM

DESCRIPTION: Elongated rhizomes with 1-inch pseudobulbs with one or two fleshy leaves; reddish flowers.

REMARKS: Not as handsome as above but unusual. Grow on tree fern slab.

SIZE: To 10 inches

TEMPERATURE: 72°–85°F

HUMIDITY: 50 percent

WATERING: Keep evenly moist

LIGHT: Sun

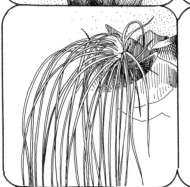

BULBOPHYLLUM LOBBII

DESCRIPTION: Fleshy leaves, large flowers, yellow marked with red.

REMARKS: Easiest of the bulbophyllums to grow. Likes moisture; grow on tree fern slab.

SIZE: To 8 inches

TEMPERATURE: 72°–85°F

HUMIDITY: 50 percent

WATERING: Keep evenly moist

LIGHT: Sun

BULBOPHYLLUM MEDUSAE

DESCRIPTION: Orchid with creeping rhizome and small single-leaved pseudobulbs; threadlike flowers.

REMARKS: Remarkable plant with exotic flowers; likes good air circulation.

SIZE: To 10 inches

TEMPERATURE: 72°–85°F

HUMIDITY: 50 percent

WATERING: Keep evenly moist

LIGHT: Shade

BULBOPHYLLUM MORPHOLOGORUM

DESCRIPTION: Tiny yellow-brown flowers, about a hundred to a cluster; pendant stem.

REMARKS: Tiny flowers but hundreds to a stem; keep somewhat dry.

SIZE: To 4 inches

TEMPERATURE: 72°–85°F

HUMIDITY: 50 percent

WATERING: Keep evenly moist

LIGHT: Shade

CALADIUM HUMBOLDTII

DESCRIPTION: Tiny light green leaves with transparent white areas between veins.

REMARKS: Keep out of sun. When leaves fade, dry out and store in pot in shady place. In three or four months start corms in fresh soil.

SIZE: To 12 inches

TEMPERATURE: 55°–70°F

HUMIDITY: 20–30 percent

WATERING: Keep quite moist

LIGHT: Bright

CALADIUM 'LITTLE RASCAL'

DESCRIPTION: Small lance-leaf, pink to light red, transversed by red to purplish veins, outer edge green and frilled.
REMARKS: Handsome hybrid; dry out when leaves fade and store dry in pot for three to four months. Start again in fresh soil.

SIZE: To 10 inches

TEMPERATURE: 55°–70°F

HUMIDITY: 20–30 percent

WATERING: Keep quite moist

LIGHT: Bright

CALADIUM 'RED CHIEF'

DESCRIPTION: Typical lance-shaped leaves, striking red.

REMARKS: Handsome hybrid; dry out when leaves fade and store dry in pot for three to four months. Start again in fresh soil.

SIZE: To 12 inches

TEMPERATURE: 55°–70°F

HUMIDITY: 20–30 percent

WATERING: Keep quite moist

LIGHT: Bright

CALATHEA BACHEMIANA

DESCRIPTION: Gray-green leaves marked dark green.

REMARKS: Grows best with good air circulation. Makes handsome plant. Grows slowly.

SIZE: To 16 inches

TEMPERATURE: 72°–80°F

HUMIDITY: 30–40 percent

WATERING: Keep quite moist

LIGHT: Shade

CALATHEA LEOPARDINA

DESCRIPTION: Tapering leaves, pale pink and dark green with brown markings.

REMARKS: Variegated leaves; makes nice table or desk accent.

SIZE: To 12 inches

TEMPERATURE: 72°–80°F

HUMIDITY: 30–40 percent

WATERING: Keep quite moist

LIGHT: Shade

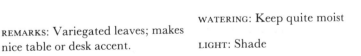

CALATHEA MICANS

DESCRIPTION: Narrow pointed leaves, medium green with a flame-shaped silvery-white center band above.

REMARKS: One of the smallest calatheas; excellent for terrariums.

SIZE: To 10 inches

TEMPERATURE: 72°–80°F

HUMIDITY: 30–40 percent

WATERING: Keep quite moist

LIGHT: Shade

CALATHEA PICTURATA ARGENTEA

DESCRIPTION: Short-stalked leaves almost silver except for a border of dark green; wine-red beneath.

REMARKS: Exquisite foliage plant; good for north windows.

SIZE: To 12 inches

TEMPERATURE: 72°–80°F

HUMIDITY: 30–40 percent

WATERING: Keep quite moist

LIGHT: Shade

CALATHEA ROSEO-PICTA

DESCRIPTION: Leaves dark green with red midrib and bright red markings fading to silvery-pink; lower surface purple.

REMARKS: The best calathea; easier to grow than others.

SIZE: To 12 inches

TEMPERATURE: 72°–80°F

HUMIDITY: 30–40 percent

WATERING: Keep quite moist

LIGHT: Shade

CALLOPSIS VOLKENSI

DESCRIPTION: Large deep green leaves, small spathelike yellow flowers.

REMARKS: Not often seen but a beauty; resembles a calla lily.

SIZE: To 6 inches

TEMPERATURE: 75°–85°F

HUMIDITY: 40 percent

WATERING: Keep evenly moist

LIGHT: Shade

CAMPANULA ELATINES (star-of-Bethlehem)

DESCRIPTION: Small round dark green leaves and handsome blue flowers.

REMARKS: Growth declines in winter; cut back to 4 or 5 inches and keep somewhat dry; start again in spring; repot.

SIZE: To 10 inches

TEMPERATURE: 55°–70°F

HUMIDITY: 20–30 percent

WATERING: Dry out between waterings

LIGHT: Bright

CAMPTOSORUS RHIZOPHYLLUS (walking fern)

DESCRIPTION: Dark green spear-shaped leaves on short stems.

REMARKS: A delightful fern; ideal for terrariums or dish gardens.

SIZE: To 3 inches

TEMPERATURE: 55°–70°F

HUMIDITY: 20–30 percent

WATERING: Keep evenly moist

LIGHT: Shade

CARISSA GRANDIFLORA 'NANA' (natal plum)

DESCRIPTION: Leathery glossy leaves and tubular pure white flowers.

SIZE: To 16 inches

TEMPERATURE: 55°–70°F

HUMIDITY: 20–30 percent

WATERING: Keep evenly moist

LIGHT: Sun

REMARKS: Water sparingly when plants rest in winter.

CATASETUM RUSSELLIANUM

DESCRIPTION: Pseudobulbs bearing plaited leaves, showy pendant green and white flowers.

SIZE: To 10 inches

TEMPERATURE: 65°–80°F

HUMIDITY: 40–50 percent

WATERING: Keep evenly moist

LIGHT: Sun

REMARKS: Pot in equal parts fir bark and soil; grow in hanging container.

CATOPSIS FLORIBUNDA

DESCRIPTION: Tubular bromeliad, dark green broad leaves, white flowers.

SIZE: To 14 inches

TEMPERATURE: 72°–80°F

HUMIDITY: 30–40 percent

WATERING: Keep evenly moist

LIGHT: Bright

REMARKS: Unusual bromeliad; adapts well to indoor culture.

CATOPSIS MORRENIANA

DESCRIPTION: Dark green leaves with brown markings, yellow and white flowers.

SIZE: To 16 inches

TEMPERATURE: 72°–80°F

HUMIDITY: 30–40 percent

WATERING: Keep evenly moist

LIGHT: Bright

REMARKS: Handsome variegated leaves; vase-shaped. Easy to grow.

CATOPSIS NUTANS

DESCRIPTION: Green spreading leaves, whitish beneath; yellow flowers.

SIZE: To 10 inches

TEMPERATURE: 72°–80°F

HUMIDITY: 30–40 percent

WATERING: Keep evenly moist

LIGHT: Bright

REMARKS: Small and charming; likes good air circulation.

100

CATTLEYA AURANTIACA

DESCRIPTION: Stiff fleshy leaves, clusters of magenta flowers.

REMARKS: Needs plenty of sun and good air circulation.

SIZE: To 14 inches

TEMPERATURE: 72°–80°F

HUMIDITY: 30–40 percent

WATERING: Keep evenly moist

LIGHT: Sun

CATTLEYA CITRINA

DESCRIPTION: Orchid with strap-shaped leaves, fragrant bell-like flowers, bright lemon.

REMARKS: Grow on tree fern slab; exquisite yellow flowers.

SIZE: To 8 inches

TEMPERATURE: 72°–80°F

HUMIDITY: 30–40 percent

WATERING: Keep evenly moist

LIGHT: Sun

CATTLEYA DOLOSA

DESCRIPTION: One or two stiff fleshy leaves; flowers magenta with yellow disc in the lip.

REMARKS: Perfectly charming small orchid; likes good air circulation; grow on fir bark.

SIZE: To 8 inches

TEMPERATURE: 72°–80°F

HUMIDITY: 30–40 percent

WATERING: Keep evenly moist

LIGHT: Sun

CATTLEYA LUTEOLA

DESCRIPTION: Orchid with solitary leaves on clustered pseudobulbs; small lemon yellow flowers.

REMARKS: Easy to grow; blooms easily. Grow on fir bark.

SIZE: To 6 inches

TEMPERATURE: 72°–80°F

HUMIDITY: 30–40 percent

WATERING: Keep evenly moist

LIGHT: Sun

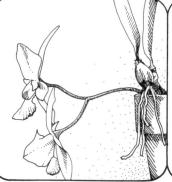

CATTLEYA WALKERIANA

DESCRIPTION: Orchid with pseudobulbs 2 to 4 inches long; one or two stiff fleshy leaves; rose-colored blooms.

REMARKS: Grow on tree fern slab; blooms in winter; very desirable.

SIZE: To 6 inches

TEMPERATURE: 72°–80°F

HUMIDITY: 30–40 percent

WATERING: Keep evenly moist

LIGHT: Sun

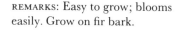
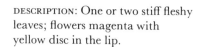
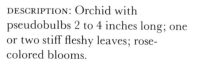

CEPHALOCEREUS PALMERI (wooly torch)

DESCRIPTION: Hardy plant with short blue-green spines and tufts of white, wooly hair.

REMARKS: Needs good sun to bloom. Rest with little water and cooler temperatures in winter.

SIZE: To 14 inches

TEMPERATURE: 72°–80°F

HUMIDITY: 20–30 percent

WATERING: Keep evenly moist

LIGHT: Sun

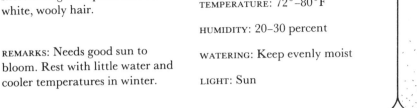

CEPHALOCEREUS POLYLOPHUS (Aztec column)

DESCRIPTION: Slow growing, columnar with fluted ribs, yellow-brown spines.

REMARKS: Needs good sun to bloom. Rest with little water and cooler temperatures in winter.

SIZE: To 16 inches

TEMPERATURE: 72°–80°F

HUMIDITY: 20–30 percent

WATERING: Keep evenly moist

LIGHT: Sun

CEPHALOCEREUS SENILIS (old man cactus)

DESCRIPTION: Ribbed columnar growth, spines hidden in long white hairs.

REMARKS: Very popular; more an oddity than a beauty.

SIZE: To 12 inches

TEMPERATURE: 72°–80°F

HUMIDITY: 20–30 percent

WATERING: Keep evenly moist

LIGHT: Sun

CEROPEGIA CAFFORUM

DESCRIPTION: Succulent leaves with silver-white veining, green flowers with purple lines.

REMARKS: Makes nice hanging basket plant. Needs good air circulation.

SIZE: To 12 inches (pendant)

TEMPERATURE: 72°–80°F

HUMIDITY: 20–30 percent

WATERING: Keep evenly moist

LIGHT: Bright

CEROPEGIA WOODII (string-of-hearts)

DESCRIPTION: Succulent heart-shaped bluish leaves marbled silver; purple flowers.

REMARKS: Makes nice hanging basket plant. Needs good air circulation.

SIZE: To 12 inches (pendant)

TEMPERATURE: 72°–80°F

HUMIDITY: 20–30 percent

WATERING: Keep evenly moist

LIGHT: Bright

102

CHAMAECEREUS SILVESTRI (peanut cactus)

DESCRIPTION: Dense clusters of short green branches; red flowers.

SIZE: To 10 inches

TEMPERATURE: 72°–80°F

HUMIDITY: 20 percent

WATERING: Keep evenly moist

REMARKS: One of the best indoor cacti; blooms in summer with minimum care.

LIGHT: Sun

CHAMAERANTHEMUM GAUDICHAUDII

DESCRIPTION: Variegated leaves, tiny white flowers.

SIZE: To 6 inches

TEMPERATURE: 75°–85°F

HUMIDITY: 30 percent

WATERING: Keep evenly moist

REMARKS: A handsome foliage plant not often seen but worth a spot in the indoor garden.

LIGHT: Shade

CHAMAERANTHEMUM IGNEUM

DESCRIPTION: Velvet textured leaves, brownish-green with red and yellow veins.

SIZE: To 14 inches

TEMPERATURE: 75°–85°F

HUMIDITY: 40 percent

WATERING: Keep evenly moist

REMARKS: Likes moisture and warmth.

LIGHT: Bright

CHAMAERANTHEMUM VENOSUM

DESCRIPTION: Small, hard leaves with silver net pattern.

SIZE: To 10 inches

TEMPERATURE: 75°–85°F

HUMIDITY: 40 percent

WATERING: Keep evenly moist

REMARKS: Easiest in group to grow.

LIGHT: Bright

CHIONODOXA LUCILAE

DESCRIPTION: Grassy leaves, bright blue flowers with white center.

SIZE: To 10 inches

TEMPERATURE: 55°–70°F

HUMIDITY: 20–30 percent

WATERING: Keep evenly moist

REMARKS: Delightful small bulbous plant; used for cut flowers.

LIGHT: Sun

CHIONODOXA SARDENIS

DESCRIPTION: Grassy leaves, bright purple flowers.

REMARKS: Start bulbs anytime during year.

SIZE: To 8 inches

TEMPERATURE: 55°–70°F

HUMIDITY: 20–30 percent

WATERING: Keep evenly moist

LIGHT: Sun

CHIONODOXA TMOLI

DESCRIPTION: Grassy leaves and vivid blue flowers.

REMARKS: Start bulbs anytime during year.

SIZE: To 6 inches

TEMPERATURE: 55°–70°F

HUMIDITY: 20–30 percent

WATERING: Keep evenly moist

LIGHT: Sun

CHRYSANTHEMUM FRUTESCENS (florist chrysanthemum)

DESCRIPTION: Leafy plant, gray-green with handsome white flowers.

REMARKS: Good for only a few months but worth the space because of handsome flowers.

SIZE: To 12 inches

TEMPERATURE: 70°–80°F

HUMIDITY: 20–30 percent

WATERING: Keep very moist

LIGHT: Sun

CIRRHOPETALUM CUMINGII

DESCRIPTION: Four-angled pseudobulb tipped with a thick solitary leaf; flowers ruby red.

REMARKS: An exquisite orchid; blooms in fall. Grow in fir bark.

SIZE: To 2 inches

TEMPERATURE: 72°–80°F

HUMIDITY: 30–40 percent

WATERING: Keep evenly moist

LIGHT: Sun

CIRRHOPETALUM LONGISSIMUM

DESCRIPTION: Fat pseudobulbs with fleshy leaf; soft pink and buff flowers.

REMARKS: Unusual flowers; grow this orchid on tree fern slab.

SIZE: To 10 inches

TEMPERATURE: 72°–80°F

HUMIDITY: 30 percent

WATERING: Keep evenly moist

LIGHT: Bright

CIRRHOPETALUM MAKOYANUM

DESCRIPTION: Single leathery dark green leaves, multicolored flowers.

SIZE: To 6 inches

TEMPERATURE: 72°–80°F

HUMIDITY: 30 percent

WATERING: Keep evenly moist

REMARKS: Blooms on and off throughout the year.

LIGHT: Bright

CIRRHOPETALUM MASTERIANUM

DESCRIPTION: Fat pseudobulb with solitary leathery leaf; tawny orange flowers.

SIZE: To 6 inches

TEMPERATURE: 72°–80°F

HUMIDITY: 30 percent

WATERING: Keep evenly moist

REMARKS: Great orchid; blooms in winter.

LIGHT: Bright

CIRRHOPETALUM ROTHSCHILDIANUM

DESCRIPTION: Single leathery leaves, pale purple-brown flowers.

SIZE: To 6 inches

TEMPERATURE: 72°–80°F

HUMIDITY: 30 percent

REMARKS: Easiest of the cirrhopetalum orchids to grow indoors.

WATERING: Keep evenly moist

LIGHT: Bright

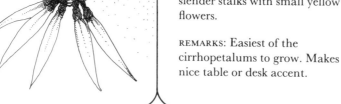

CIRRHOPETALUM ROXBURGHII

DESCRIPTION: Small pseudobulbs and solitary leaves 2 inches long; slender stalks with small yellow flowers.

SIZE: To 10 inches

TEMPERATURE: 72°–80°F

HUMIDITY: 30–40 percent

WATERING: Keep evenly moist

REMARKS: Easiest of the cirrhopetalums to grow. Makes nice table or desk accent.

LIGHT: Sun

CITRUS MITIS

DESCRIPTION: Leafy plant; bright green, white flowers.

SIZE: To 20 inches

TEMPERATURE: 70°–80°F

HUMIDITY: 20–30 percent

WATERING: Keep evenly moist

REMARKS: Mist leaves frequently; likes good air circulation.

LIGHT: Sun

CITRUS TAITENSIS (otaheite orange)

DESCRIPTION: Glossy green dense foliage and few spines, waxy white fragrant flowers.

REMARKS: Nice small branching tree. Mist with water frequently.

SIZE: To 20 inches

TEMPERATURE: 70°–80°F

HUMIDITY: 20–30 percent

WATERING: Keep evenly moist

LIGHT: Sun

CLEISTOCACTUS BAUMANNII (scarlet bugler)

DESCRIPTION: Stiff stems topped with white spines; long-blooming bright red tubular flowers.

REMARKS: Good indoor cactus; robust. Dry out somewhat in winter.

SIZE: To 16 inches

TEMPERATURE: 72°–80°F

HUMIDITY: 20–30 percent

WATERING: Keep evenly moist

LIGHT: Sun

CLEISTOCACTUS STRAUSII (silver torch)

DESCRIPTION: Columnar clustering variety, silver-haired; dark red flowers.

REMARKS: Good indoor cactus; robust. Dry out somewhat in winter.

SIZE: To 16 inches

TEMPERATURE: 72°–80°F

HUMIDITY: 20–30 percent

WATERING: Keep evenly moist

LIGHT: Sun

COELOGYNE CRISTATA

DESCRIPTION: Pear-shaped pseudobulbs with one or two leaves; flowers white with yellow-stained lip.

REMARKS: Needs a severe drying out in fall to bloom. Grow almost dry for three to four weeks.

SIZE: To 10 inches

TEMPERATURE: 65°–78°F

HUMIDITY: 30–40 percent

WATERING: Keep evenly moist

LIGHT: Shade

COELOGYNE OCHRACEA

DESCRIPTION: Pear-shaped pseudobulbs with one or two leaves; fragrant white flowers bordered with orange.

REMARKS: Blooms on and off throughout the warm months.

SIZE: To 10 inches

TEMPERATURE: 65°–78°F

HUMIDITY: 30–40 percent

WATERING: Keep evenly moist

LIGHT: Shade

COLCHICUM AUTUMNALE (autumn crocus)

DESCRIPTION: Lance-shaped leaves; flowers purple to white.

SIZE: To 6 inches

TEMPERATURE: 65°–78°F

HUMIDITY: 20–30 percent

REMARKS: Makes nice pot plant; start corms in fall.

WATERING: Keep evenly moist

LIGHT: Bright

COLCHICUM BULBOCODIUM (meadow saffron)

DESCRIPTION: Lance-shaped leaves; blue flowers.

SIZE: To 6 inches

TEMPERATURE: 65°–78°F

HUMIDITY: 20–30 percent

REMARKS: Makes nice pot plant; start corms in fall.

WATERING: Keep evenly moist

LIGHT: Bright

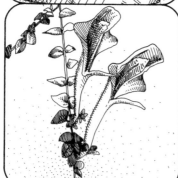

COLUMNEA MICROPHYLLA

DESCRIPTION: Soft trailing plant with tiny rounded or broad-elliptic coppery hairy leaves; orange flowers.

SIZE: To 10 inches (pendant)

TEMPERATURE: 72°–80°F

HUMIDITY: 20–30 percent

REMARKS: Makes handsome basket plant; needs some pampering.

WATERING: Keep evenly moist

LIGHT: Bright

CONVALLARIA MAJALIS (lily-of-the-valley)

DESCRIPTION: Broad green leaves and bell-shaped white fragrant flowers.

SIZE: To 8 inches

TEMPERATURE: 65°–75°F

HUMIDITY: 20–30 percent

REMARKS: Good indoor plant; start corms in 8-inch pots in fall.

WATERING: Keep evenly moist

LIGHT: Bright

COPTIS TRIFOLIA (goldenthread)

DESCRIPTION: Dainty plant with handsome scalloped leaves, yellow flowers.

SIZE: To 8 inches

TEMPERATURE: 55°–70°F

HUMIDITY: 20–30 percent

REMARKS: Interesting wildflower that grows for several months indoors.

WATERING: Keep evenly moist

LIGHT: Shade

COTYLEDON TOMENTOSA

DESCRIPTION: Gray-green egg-shaped leaves covered with white down; yellow flowers.

REMARKS: A better houseplant than most people think; rest somewhat dry in winter.

SIZE: To 12 inches

TEMPERATURE: 72°–80°F

HUMIDITY: 20–30 percent

WATERING: Keep evenly moist

LIGHT: Bright

CRASSULA ARBORESCENS (silver dollar plant)

DESCRIPTION: Large silvery leaves with red margins.

REMARKS: Makes nice branching plant; rest somewhat in winter.

SIZE: To 14 inches

TEMPERATURE: 72°–80°F

HUMIDITY: 20–30 percent

WATERING: Keep evenly moist

LIGHT: Bright

CRASSULA BARBATA

DESCRIPTION: Low-growing with green leaves fringed with white hairs.

REMARKS: Dies down after flowering but comes back.

SIZE: To 5 inches

TEMPERATURE: 72°–80°F

HUMIDITY: 20–30 percent

WATERING: Keep evenly moist

LIGHT: Bright

CRASSULA DELTOIDEA (silver beads)

DESCRIPTION: Low-growing with fleshy white triangular leaves.

REMARKS: Nice easy plant to grow. Rest somewhat dry in winter.

SIZE: To 14 inches

TEMPERATURE: 72°–80°F

HUMIDITY: 20–30 percent

WATERING: Keep evenly moist

LIGHT: Bright

CRASSULA SCHMIDTII

DESCRIPTION: Fleshy needlelike channeled leaves gray-green with darker dots; clusters of carmine-red flowers.

REMARKS: Good table or desk plant. Grows easily indoors.

SIZE: To 6 inches

TEMPERATURE: 72°–80°F

HUMIDITY: 20–30 percent

WATERING: Keep evenly moist

LIGHT: Bright

CRASSULA TERES

DESCRIPTION: Tightly packed column of pale green leaves.

SIZE: To 6 inches (pendant)

TEMPERATURE: 72°–80°F

HUMIDITY: 20–30 percent

REMARKS: Unusual and excellent for indoors. Keep water off the leaves.

WATERING: Keep evenly moist

LIGHT: Bright

CROCUS CANCELLATUS

DESCRIPTION: Thick, hard leaves, white or purple flowers.

SIZE: To 6 inches

TEMPERATURE: 55°–70°F

HUMIDITY: 20–30 percent

REMARKS: Start bulbs in fall in 8-inch pots.

WATERING: Keep evenly moist

LIGHT: Bright

CROCUS CHRYSANTHUS

DESCRIPTION: Spathelike leaves, usually yellow flowers.

SIZE: To 10 inches

TEMPERATURE: 55°–70°F

HUMIDITY: 20–30 percent

REMARKS: Start bulbs in fall in 8-inch pots.

WATERING: Keep evenly moist

LIGHT: Bright

CROCUS SIEBERI

DESCRIPTION: Spathelike leaves, dark purple to white flowers.

SIZE: To 6 inches

TEMPERATURE: 55°–70°F

HUMIDITY: 20–30 percent

REMARKS: The best crocus for indoors.

WATERING: Keep evenly moist

LIGHT: Bright

CROCUS TOMASINIANUS

DESCRIPTION: Spathelike leaves, lavender flowers.

SIZE: To 8 inches

TEMPERATURE: 55°–70°F

HUMIDITY: 20–30 percent

REMARKS: Start bulbs in fall in pots for spring bloom.

WATERING: Keep evenly moist

LIGHT: Bright

109

CROCUS VERNA

DESCRIPTION: Spathelike leaves, white to lilac or purple flowers.

SIZE: To 8 inches

TEMPERATURE: 55°–70°F

HUMIDITY: 20–30 percent

WATERING: Keep evenly moist

LIGHT: Bright

REMARKS: Start bulbs in fall in pots for spring bloom.

CROSSANDRA INFUNDIBULIFORMIS

DESCRIPTION: Bright shiny leaves and clusters of orange flowers.

SIZE: To 14 inches

TEMPERATURE: 72°–80°F

HUMIDITY: 20–30 percent

WATERING: Keep evenly moist

LIGHT: Bright

REMARKS: Blooms when young; mist foliage occasionally.

CRYPTANTHUS ACAULIS

DESCRIPTION: Green leaves, white flowers.

SIZE: To 6 inches

TEMPERATURE: 72°–80°F

HUMIDITY: 20–30 percent

WATERING: Keep evenly moist

LIGHT: Bright

REMARKS: Handsome foliage plant; grows easily.

CRYPTANTHUS BEUCKERI

DESCRIPTION: Leaves greenish-cream; flowers white.

SIZE: To 10 inches

TEMPERATURE: 72°–80°F

HUMIDITY: 20–30 percent

WATERING: Keep evenly moist

LIGHT: Bright

REMARKS: Handsome foliage plant; grows easily.

CRYPTANTHUS BROMELIATUS

DESCRIPTION: Leaves pinkish-brown; silver-green white flowers.

SIZE: To 12 inches

TEMPERATURE: 72°–80°F

HUMIDITY: 20–30 percent

WATERING: Keep evenly moist

LIGHT: Bright

REMARKS: Easy to grow; excellent leaf color.

CRYPTANTHUS BROMELIOIDES 'TRICOLOR'

DESCRIPTION: Leaves greenish-brown; flowers white.

SIZE: To 8 inches

TEMPERATURE: 72°–80°F

HUMIDITY: 20–30 percent

REMARKS: One of the best hybrids; stellar leaf color.

WATERING: Keep evenly moist

LIGHT: Bright

CRYPTANTHUS TERMINALIS

DESCRIPTION: Leaves greenish-brown; white flowers.

SIZE: To 8 inches

TEMPERATURE: 72°–80°F

HUMIDITY: 20–30 percent

REMARKS: Not spectacular but easy to grow.

WATERING: Keep evenly moist

LIGHT: Bright

CRYPTANTHUS ZONATUS

DESCRIPTION: Wavy lance-shaped brownish-green leaves, tiny white flowers.

size: To 5 inches

TEMPERATURE: 70°–80°F

HUMIDITY: 30 percent

REMARKS: A very amenable bromeliad; nice color.

WATERING: Keep somewhat dry

LIGHT: Sun

CTENANTHE OPPENHEIMIANA

DESCRIPTION: Dark green leaves with gray bands; purple beneath.

SIZE: To 14 inches

TEMPERATURE: 72°–80°F

HUMIDITY: 40 percent

REMARKS: Variegated plant; handsome but difficult to grow.

WATERING: Keep evenly moist

LIGHT: Shade

CTENANTHE OPPENHEIMIANA 'TRICOLOR'

DESCRIPTION: Dark green leaves with gray bands, purple beneath; cream-colored markings.

SIZE: To 12 inches

TEMPERATURE: 72°–80°F

HUMIDITY: 30–40 percent

REMARKS: Exquisite leaf color; likes good ventilation.

WATERING: Keep evenly moist

LIGHT: Shade

CTENANTHE SETOSA

DESCRIPTION: Green leafy plant; white flowers.

SIZE: To 20 inches

TEMPERATURE: 72°–80°F

HUMIDITY: 30–40 percent

WATERING: Keep evenly moist

LIGHT: Shade

REMARKS: Lush-looking plant somewhat difficult to grow.

CUPHEA HYSSOPIFOLIA

DESCRIPTION: Tiny linear leathery leaves, green flowers, six petals, purplish-rose.

SIZE: To 12 inches

TEMPERATURE: 72°–80°F

HUMIDITY: 30–40 percent

WATERING: Keep evenly moist

LIGHT: Shade

REMARKS: Blooms on and off throughout the summer.

CYANOTIS SOMALIENSE (pussy ears)

DESCRIPTION: Succulent little creeper, glossy green leaves covered with soft white hair; purple and orange flowers.

SIZE: To 12 inches

TEMPERATURE: 70°–78°F

HUMIDITY: 20–30 percent

WATERING: Keep evenly moist

LIGHT: Bright

REMARKS: Dies down in winter; let rest in shade until spring.

CYCLAMEN COUM

DESCRIPTION: Heart-shaped dark green leaves, usually lavender flowers.

SIZE: To 10 inches

TEMPERATURE: 70°–80°F

HUMIDITY: 20–30 percent

WATERING: Keep evenly moist

LIGHT: Bright

REMARKS: Rest for three to four months after flowering; start again in fresh soil.

CYCLAMEN PERSICUM

DESCRIPTION: Heart-shaped bluish leaves with silvery pattern.

SIZE: To 10 inches

TEMPERATURE: 70°–80°F

HUMIDITY: 20–30 percent

WATERING: Keep evenly moist

LIGHT: Bright

REMARKS: Rest for three to four months after flowering; start again in fresh soil.

CYMBALARIA MURALIS (kenilworth ivy)

DESCRIPTION: Fresh green waxy leaves; ground cover growth.

SIZE: To 6 inches

TEMPERATURE: 70°–80°F

HUMIDITY: 20–30 percent

REMARKS: Rest for three to four months after flowering; start again in fresh soil.

WATERING: Keep evenly moist

LIGHT: Bright

CYPRIPEDIUM ACAULE

DESCRIPTION: Straplike leaves in fan shape.

SIZE: To 12 inches

TEMPERATURE: 65°–78°F

HUMIDITY: 30–40 percent

REMARKS: Easy to grow orchid; likes good air circulation.

WATERING: Keep evenly moist

LIGHT: Bright

CYPRIPEDIUM BELLATUM

DESCRIPTION: Dark green or mottled strap foliage, fan formation; white or pale yellow flowers marked with purple spots.

SIZE: To 14 inches

TEMPERATURE: 65°–78°F

HUMIDITY: 30–40 percent

REMARKS: Easy to grow orchid; likes good air circulation.

WATERING: Keep evenly moist

LIGHT: Bright

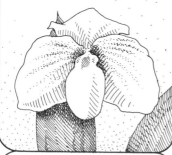
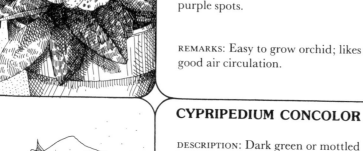

CYPRIPEDIUM CONCOLOR

DESCRIPTION: Dark green or mottled strap foliage; flowers yellow specked with crimson dots.

SIZE: To 6 inches

TEMPERATURE: 65°–78°F

HUMIDITY: 30–40 percent

REMARKS: One of the best lady-slippers; dependable to bloom every year.

WATERING: Keep evenly moist

LIGHT: Bright

CYPRIPEDIUM INSIGNE

DESCRIPTION: Dark green or mottled strap foliage; flowers brown-veined apple green, waxy texture.

SIZE: To 12 inches

TEMPERATURE: 65°–78°F

HUMIDITY: 30–40 percent

REMARKS: Good winter bloomer; dependable.

WATERING: Keep evenly moist

LIGHT: Bright

CYPRIPEDIUM NIVEUM

DESCRIPTION: Dark green or mottled strap foliage, satiny white flowers speckled purple.

REMARKS: Good small orchid; robust and pretty.

SIZE: To 6 inches

TEMPERATURE: 65°–78°F

HUMIDITY: 30–40 percent

WATERING: Keep evenly moist

LIGHT: Bright

CYPRIPEDIUM PARVIFLORUM (ladyslipper orchid)

DESCRIPTION: Broad green creased leaves; yellow flowers tinged brown.

REMARKS: One of the wild species; somewhat difficult to grow indoors.

SIZE: To 14 inches

TEMPERATURE: 65°–78°F

HUMIDITY: 30–40 percent

WATERING: Keep evenly moist

LIGHT: Bright

CYPRIPEDIUM PUBESCENS (ladyslipper orchid)

DESCRIPTION: Broad green creased leaves; yellow flowers tinged brown.

REMARKS: One of the wild species; somewhat difficult to grow indoors.

SIZE: To 10 inches

TEMPERATURE: 65°–78°F

HUMIDITY: 30–40 percent

WATERING: Keep evenly moist

LIGHT: Bright

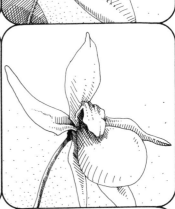

CYRTOMIUM FALCATUM (holly fern)

DESCRIPTION: Somewhat large, shiny, toothed leaves; holly-shaped.

REMARKS: Likes frequent misting; grows well in basket.

SIZE: To 14 inches

TEMPERATURE: 70°–80°F

HUMIDITY: 20–30 percent

WATERING: Keep evenly moist

LIGHT: Bright

DAVALLIA BULLATA MARIESII (rabbit's foot fern)

DESCRIPTION: Creeping brown rhizomes, lacy fronds; very graceful.

REMARKS: Handsome plant but needs attention; do not get water on scaly surface rhizomes.

SIZE: To 10 inches

TEMPERATURE: 60°–75°F

HUMIDITY: 20–30 percent

WATERING: Keep evenly moist

LIGHT: Bright

DENDROBIUM AGGREGATUM

DESCRIPTION: Prominent pseudo-bulbs with pendant spikes of small, scented, vivid yellow flowers.
REMARKS: Handsome orchid that needs a four- to six-week rest after flowering; only resume watering when new growth starts; otherwise, keep evenly moist.

SIZE: To 10 inches

TEMPERATURE: 70°–80°F

HUMIDITY: 30–40 percent

WATERING: See remarks

LIGHT: Sun

DENDROBIUM FARMERI

DESCRIPTION: Small succulent leaves and handsome large white flowers with yellow throat.
REMARKS: Grow in fir bark; must have winter rest, almost dry for three weeks to produce spring flowers; otherwise, keep evenly moist.

SIZE: To 12 inches

TEMPERATURE: 70°–80°F

HUMIDITY: 30–40 percent

WATERING: See remarks

LIGHT: Sun

DENDROBIUM FORMOSUM

DESCRIPTION: Small green leaves and dazzling white flowers.

REMARKS: Grow in fir bark; must have winter sun to produce spring flowers.

SIZE: To 10 inches

TEMPERATURE: 70°–80°F

HUMIDITY: 30–40 percent

WATERING: Dry out between waterings

LIGHT: Sun

DENDROBIUM KINGIANUM

DESCRIPTION: Small succulent leaves; 1-inch flowers rose-colored striped with violet.

REMARKS: Exquisite orchid; grows in fir bark. Good table or desk accent. Flowers last over a month.

SIZE: To 10 inches

TEMPERATURE: 70°–80°F

HUMIDITY: 30–40 percent

WATERING: Keep evenly moist

LIGHT: Sun

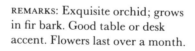

DENDROBIUM LODDIGESI

DESCRIPTION: Prominent pseudobulbs and thick green leaves, lavender pink flowers.

REMARKS: Easier to grow than most dendrobiums. Needs winter sun.

SIZE: To 12 inches

TEMPERATURE: 70°–80°F

HUMIDITY: 30–40 percent

WATERING: Dry out between waterings

LIGHT: Sun

DENDROBIUM NOBILE

DESCRIPTION: Leafy canes; deciduous plant with purple and white flowers.

REMARKS: Dry out in late summer to encourage flower buds; stellar orchid.

SIZE: To 14 inches (trailing)

TEMPERATURE: 70°–80°F

HUMIDITY: 30 percent

WATERING: See remarks

LIGHT: Sun

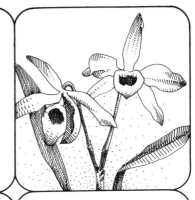

DIANTHUS ALPINUS

DESCRIPTION: Grassy green leaves, small bearded red-purple flowers speckled white.

REMARKS: This outdoor plant is tough to grow indoors but worth the effort.

SIZE: To 6 inches

TEMPERATURE: 55°–65°F

HUMIDITY: 30 percent

WATERING: Keep quite moist

LIGHT: Sun

DIANTHUS 'BO PEEP'

DESCRIPTION: Grassy-type foliage; white flowers streaked pink.

REMARKS: Tough to grow indoors but the flowers are worth the effort.

SIZE: To 6 inches

TEMPERATURE: 55°–65°F

HUMIDITY: 30 percent

WATERING: Keep quite moist

LIGHT: Sun

DIANTHUS PLUMARIUS

DESCRIPTION: Short grassy leaves, purple flowers.

REMARKS: This outdoor plant is tough to bloom indoors but worth the effort. Grow in 8-inch pot.

SIZE: To 8 inches

TEMPERATURE: 55°–65°F

HUMIDITY: 30 percent

WATERING: Keep wet

LIGHT: Sun

DIONAEA MUSCIPULA (Venus flytrap)

DESCRIPTION: Carnivorous rosette with long teeth which close traplike.

REMARKS: A curiosity and difficult to grow unless in a terrarium.

SIZE: To 3 inches

TEMPERATURE: 75°–85°F

HUMIDITY: 60–70 percent

WATERING: Keep wet

LIGHT: Shade

DROSERA ROTUNDIFOLIA (sundew)

DESCRIPTION: Small herb with flat hairy petioles, round hairy leaves; small white flowers.

REMARKS: Unusual, difficult.

SIZE: To 4 inches

TEMPERATURE: 75°–85°F

HUMIDITY: 50 percent

WATERING: Keep very moist

LIGHT: Sun

DYCKIA BREVIFOLIA

DESCRIPTION: Leaves dark green; flowers orange.

REMARKS: Spiny and not too attractive but valued for its orange flowers.

SIZE: To 10 inches

TEMPERATURE: 72°–80°F

HUMIDITY: 30 percent

WATERING: Keep evenly moist

LIGHT: Sun

DYCKIA RARIFLORA

DESCRIPTION: Leaves silver-gray; flowers orange.

REMARKS: Needs little attention and does well indoors.

SIZE: To 10 inches

TEMPERATURE: 72°–80°F

HUMIDITY: 30 percent

WATERING: Keep evenly moist

LIGHT: Sun

ECHEVERIA DERENBERGII (painted lady)

DESCRIPTION: Thick pale green rosette with red leaf margins.

REMARKS: Undemanding succulent that bears orange flowers in the dull days.

SIZE: To 14 inches

TEMPERATURE: 70°–78°F

HUMIDITY: 30 percent

WATERING: Keep evenly moist

LIGHT: Sun

ECHEVERIA 'DORIS TAYLOR'

DESCRIPTION: Thick succulent gray-green leaves, edged red.

REMARKS: Exquisite foliage plant; do not get water on leaves.

SIZE: To 12 inches

TEMPERATURE: 70°–78°F

HUMIDITY: 30 percent

WATERING: Keep evenly moist

LIGHT: Sun

ECHEVERIA ELEGANS (Mexican snowball)

DESCRIPTION: Clustering rosette of light blue-green leaves frosted white.

REMARKS: Exquisite leaves and easy to grow. Do not get water on leaves.

SIZE: To 16 inches

TEMPERATURE: 70°–78°F

HUMIDITY: 30 percent

WATERING: Keep evenly moist

LIGHT: Sun

ECHEVERIA HAAGEANA

DESCRIPTION: Loose open rosette; leaves edged pink.

REMARKS: Exquisite leaves and easy to grow. Do not get water on leaves.

SIZE: To 10 inches

TEMPERATURE: 70°–78°F

HUMIDITY: 30 percent

WATERING: Keep evenly moist

LIGHT: Sun

ECHEVERIA PULVINATA

DESCRIPTION: Rounded leaves, red flowers.

REMARKS: Exquisite leaves and easy to grow. Do not get water on leaves.

SIZE: To 14 inches

TEMPERATURE: 70°–78°F

HUMIDITY: 30 percent

WATERING: Keep evenly moist

LIGHT: Sun

ECHEVERIA SIMULANS

DESCRIPTION: Fleshy light green leaves, reddish-yellow flowers.

REMARKS: Beautiful foliage plant for indoors.

SIZE: To 8 inches

TEMPERATURE: 70°–80°F

HUMIDITY: 20 percent

WATERING: Keep evenly moist

LIGHT: Bright

ECHEVERIA TOLUCENSIS

DESCRIPTION: Blue-green rosette of leaves; yellow flowers striped red.

REMARKS: Handsome foliage plant.

SIZE: To 8 inches

TEMPERATURE: 70°–80°F

HUMIDITY: 20 percent

WATERING: Keep evenly moist

LIGHT: Bright

ECHINOCACTUS GRUSONI (golden barrel)

DESCRIPTION: Barrel-shaped, sharp yellow spines; with age develops a crown of yellow wool.

REMARKS: Do not get water on plant; give slight winter rest with very little water.

SIZE: To 10 inches

TEMPERATURE: 72°–80°F

HUMIDITY: 30 percent

WATERING: Dry out between waterings

LIGHT: Sun

ECHINOCEREUS REICHENBACHII (lace cactus)

DESCRIPTION: Small, heavily spined plant with pink flowers.

REMARKS: Beautiful cactus; needs slight rest in winter; does well indoors.

SIZE: To 8 inches

TEMPERATURE: 72°–80°F

HUMIDITY: 30 percent

WATERING: Dry out between waterings

LIGHT: Sun

ECHINOPSIS KERMESIANA

DESCRIPTION: Rounded plant with ribs; lilylike red blooms.

REMARKS: Flowers open at night; rest somewhat in winter with less water.

SIZE: To 14 inches

TEMPERATURE: 72°–80°F

HUMIDITY: 30 percent

WATERING: Dry out between waterings

LIGHT: Sun

ECHINOPSIS MULTIPLEX (barrel cactus)

DESCRIPTION: Ribbed cactus, spiny; rose-red flowers.

REMARKS: Very handsome and easy to grow.

SIZE: To 8 inches (across)

TEMPERATURE: 72°–80°F

HUMIDITY: 30 percent

WATERING: Keep somewhat dry

LIGHT: Sun

EPIDENDRUM ATROPURPUREUM

DESCRIPTION: Egg-shaped pseudobulbs; pendant stems of chocolate brown and lavender flowers.

REMARKS: Easy to bloom orchid; flowers last for several weeks. Grow in fir bark.

SIZE: To 12 inches

TEMPERATURE: 72°–80°F

HUMIDITY: 40 percent

WATERING: Keep evenly moist

LIGHT: Sun

EPIDENDRUM CILIARE

DESCRIPTION: Graceful habit; leathery leaves, long stems that bear large lilac flowers.

REMARKS: Flowers last several weeks; grow in fir bark. Fine orchid.

SIZE: To 12 inches

TEMPERATURE: 72°–80°F

HUMIDITY: 40 percent

WATERING: Keep evenly moist

LIGHT: Sun

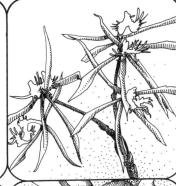

EPIDENDRUM MATTHEWSI

DESCRIPTION: Leathery leaves with small purplish flowers.

REMARKS: Flowers last several weeks; grow in fir bark. Fine small orchid.

SIZE: To 12 inches

TEMPERATURE: 72°–80°F

HUMIDITY: 40 percent

WATERING: Keep evenly moist

LIGHT: Sun

EPIDENDRUM VITTELLINUM

DESCRIPTION: Pseudobulb tipped with two leaves; arching spike bears small red flowers.

REMARKS: Difficult to bloom; give coolness (60°F) in fall to force winter flowers. Another handsome orchid.

SIZE: To 4 inches

TEMPERATURE: 72°–80°F

HUMIDITY: 40 percent

WATERING: Keep evenly moist

LIGHT: Sun

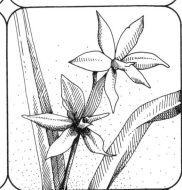

EPIGAEA REPENS (trailing arbutus)

DESCRIPTION: Deep green leathery leaves; clusters of very fragrant bell-shaped flowers with green sepals.

REMARKS: Wildflower that sometimes succeeds indoors; use rich mucky soil.

SIZE: To 10 inches

TEMPERATURE: 70°–80°F

HUMIDITY: 60 percent

WATERING: Keep wet

LIGHT: Shade

EPISCIA DIANTHIFLORA

DESCRIPTION: Green velvety leaves and tufted white flowers.

REMARKS: Likes good air circulation and a rich porous soil.

SIZE: To 10 inches

TEMPERATURE: 75°–85°F

HUMIDITY: 50 percent

WATERING: Keep evenly moist

LIGHT: Bright

EUCHARIS GRANDIFLORA (Amazon lily)

DESCRIPTION: Shiny broad green leaves and fragrant star-shaped white flowers.

REMARKS: Allow plant to rest after blooming for about three weeks, then resume watering.

SIZE: To 16 inches

TEMPERATURE: 65°–75°F

HUMIDITY: 20–30 percent

WATERING: Dry out between waterings

LIGHT: Sun

EUCOMIS PUNCTATA (pineapple plant)

DESCRIPTION: Shiny green foliage and cones of small yellow-green flowers.

REMARKS: An unusual bulbous plant that will bloom yearly with little care.

SIZE: To 16 inches

TEMPERATURE: 72°–80°F

HUMIDITY: 30 percent

WATERING: Keep evenly moist

LIGHT: Bright

EUPHORBIA OBESA (basketball plant)

DESCRIPTION: Gray-green globe marked with reddish length and across stripes; rows of small knobs along ridges.

REMARKS: More bizarre than beautiful but worth the space. Easy to grow.

SIZE: To 10 inches

TEMPERATURE: 72°–80°F

HUMIDITY: 30 percent

WATERING: Keep somewhat dry

LIGHT: Sun

EXACUM AFFINE (German violet)

DESCRIPTION: Bushy biennial with waxy ovate leaves; tiny bluish-lilac starlike fragrant flowers.

REMARKS: Blooms its head off in winter; very desirable.

SIZE: To 16 inches

TEMPERATURE: 65°–75°F

HUMIDITY: 20–30 percent

WATERING: Keep evenly moist

LIGHT: Sun

FAUCARIA SPECIOSA

DESCRIPTION: Gray-green small leaves, yellow flowers.

REMARKS: Not spectacular but very easy to grow.

SIZE: To 8 inches

TEMPERATURE: 70°–80°F

HUMIDITY: 30 percent

WATERING: Dry out between waterings

LIGHT: Sun

FAUCARIA TIGRINA

DESCRIPTION: Gray-green leaves with long slender teeth; yellow flowers.

SIZE: To 8 inches

TEMPERATURE: 70°–80°F

HUMIDITY: 30 percent

WATERING: Dry out between waterings

REMARKS: Very popular and an easy succulent plant to grow.

LIGHT: Sun

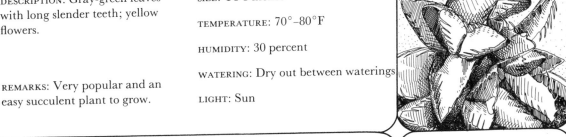

FAUCARIA TUBERCULOSA

DESCRIPTION: Triangular leaves; spreading plant, white dotted.

SIZE: To 6 inches

TEMPERATURE: 70°–80°F

HUMIDITY: 30 percent

WATERING: Dry out between waterings

REMARKS: An oddity but requires little care.

LIGHT: Sun

FELICIA AMELLOIDES

DESCRIPTION: Ovate leaves, daisylike flowers with sky-blue florets and yellow disk.

SIZE: To 16 inches

TEMPERATURE: 65°–75°F

HUMIDITY: 30 percent

REMARKS: An outdoor plant that does well indoors; has beautiful blue flowers.

WATERING: Keep wet

LIGHT: Sun

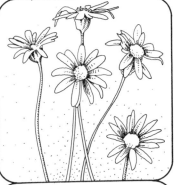

FENESTRARIA AURANTIACA (window plant)

DESCRIPTION: Circular or triangular thick leaves, orange flowers.

SIZE: To 4 inches

TEMPERATURE: 72°–80°F

HUMIDITY: 20–30 percent

WATERING: Keep somewhat dry

REMARKS: Best grown in a gravel-based soil; keep very dry in winter.

LIGHT: Sun

FENESTRARIA RHOPALOPHYLLA (window plant)

DESCRIPTION: Green triangular leaves, white flowers.

SIZE: To 4 inches

TEMPERATURE: 72°–80°F

HUMIDITY: 20–30 percent

WATERING: Keep somewhat dry

REMARKS: Best grown in a gravel-based soil; keep very dry in winter.

LIGHT: Sun

FICUS PUMILA

DESCRIPTION: Branching creeper with small dark green leaves less than 1 inch long.

REMARKS: Fast growing and an easy indoor plant; unusual and desirable.

SIZE: To 14 inches

TEMPERATURE: 70°–80°F

HUMIDITY: 30 percent

WATERING: Keep evenly moist

LIGHT: Shade

FITTONIA VERSCHAFFELTII

DESCRIPTION: Oval dark green leaves, network of deep red veins.

REMARKS: Very popular and an exquisite foliage plant. Keep water off leaves.

SIZE: To 14 inches

TEMPERATURE: 75°–85°F

HUMIDITY: 40 percent

WATERING: Dry out between waterings

LIGHT: Bright

FORTUNELLA HINDSII

DESCRIPTION: Branched shrub with green oval leaves; edible orange fruit.

REMARKS: Nice little citrus tree for indoors.

SIZE: To 18 inches

TEMPERATURE: 70°–80°F

HUMIDITY: 30 percent

WATERING: Keep wet

LIGHT: Sun

FRAGARIA INDICA

DESCRIPTION: Oval leaves, toothed, hairy underneath.

REMARKS: May bear strawberries indoors; unusual and good.

SIZE: To 12 inches

TEMPERATURE: 65°–75°F

HUMIDITY: 30 percent

WATERING: Keep evenly moist

LIGHT: Sun

FUCHSIA MEGALLONICA

DESCRIPTION: Bushy with small ovate leaves, pendulous slender flowers, purplish-red.

REMARKS: Does well indoors and very pretty; trim back somewhat each year in late winter.

SIZE: To 14 inches

TEMPERATURE: 60°–75°F

HUMIDITY: 30 percent

WATERING: Keep evenly moist

LIGHT: Shade

GALANTHUS NIVALIS

DESCRIPTION: Green broad leaves; flowers white with green markings.

REMARKS: Try in 8-inch pots indoors, use four corms to a container.

SIZE: To 8 inches

TEMPERATURE: 65°–75°F

HUMIDITY: 30 percent

WATERING: Keep evenly moist

LIGHT: Bright

GASTERIA BATESIANA

DESCRIPTION: Broad triangular olive green leaves.

REMARKS: Good succulent plant for indoors; easy to care for.

SIZE: To 8 inches

TEMPERATURE: 70°–80°F

HUMIDITY: 30 percent

WATERING: Dry out between waterings

LIGHT: Bright

GASTERIA LILIPUTANA

DESCRIPTION: Succulent with spirally, thick, short dark green leaves.

REMARKS: Fine small plant for indoors; grows slowly and easy to care for. Good for dish gardens.

SIZE: To 6 inches

TEMPERATURE: 70°–80.°F

HUMIDITY: 30 percent

WATERING: Dry out between waterings

LIGHT: Bright

GASTERIA MACULATA

DESCRIPTION: Tongue-shaped dark green glossy leaves with white spots.

REMARKS: Good accent plant for table or desk; rest slightly in winter with less water.

SIZE: To 8 inches

TEMPERATURE: 70°–80°F

HUMIDITY: 30 percent

WATERING: Dry out between waterings

LIGHT: Bright

GASTERIA TRIGONA

DESCRIPTION: Leaves spirally arranged in rows, smooth surface with small white spots in bands.

REMARKS: Good accent plant for table or desk; rest slightly in winter with less water.

SIZE: To 10 inches

TEMPERATURE: 70°–80°F

HUMIDITY: 30 percent

WATERING: Dry out between waterings

LIGHT: Bright

GASTERIA VERRUCOSA

DESCRIPTION: Tapered pink and purplish leaves with white warts.

SIZE: To 8 inches

TEMPERATURE: 70°–80°F

HUMIDITY: 30 percent

REMARKS: Most popular in group; ideal for dish gardens.

WATERING: Dry out between waterings

LIGHT: Bright

GERANIUM 'ALCYONE'

DESCRIPTION: Rich green leaves, large orange-salmon flowers.

SIZE: To 6 inches

TEMPERATURE: 65°–75°F

HUMIDITY: 30 percent

REMARKS: Blooms when only 2 inches high; try to maintain cool night-time temperatures.

WATERING: Keep evenly moist

LIGHT: Bright

GERANIUM 'ALDEBARAN'

DESCRIPTION: Small dark green leaves, rose-pink flowers.

SIZE: To 8 inches

TEMPERATURE: 60°–75°F

HUMIDITY: 30 percent

WATERING: Keep evenly moist

REMARKS: True dwarf; very pretty.

LIGHT: Bright

GERANIUM 'ALTAIR'

DESCRIPTION: Dark green leaves, salmon orange flowers.

SIZE: To 6 inches

TEMPERATURE: 60°–75°F

HUMIDITY: 30 percent

WATERING: Keep evenly moist

REMARKS: Plant needs coolness at night to prosper.

LIGHT: Bright

GERANIUM 'ANTARES'

DESCRIPTION: Dark foliage and large single flowers in dark burning scarlet.

SIZE: To 6 inches

TEMPERATURE: 65°–75°F

HUMIDITY: 30 percent

WATERING: Keep evenly moist

REMARKS: Stays small; a dependable plant.

LIGHT: Bright

GERANIUM 'BLACK VESUVIUS'

DESCRIPTION: Leaves dark olive green zoned blackish brown; large orange-scarlet single flowers.

REMARKS: Large flowers for size of plant; one of the best.

SIZE: To 4 inches

TEMPERATURE: 65°–75°F

HUMIDITY: 30 percent

WATERING: Keep evenly moist

LIGHT: Bright

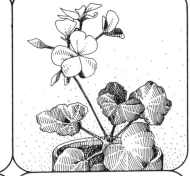

GERANIUM 'CAPELLA'

DESCRIPTION: Forest green leaves, double pink flowers.

REMARKS: Grows quickly; good robust plant.

SIZE: To 6 inches

TEMPERATURE: 65°–75°F

HUMIDITY: 30 percent

WATERING: Keep evenly moist

LIGHT: Bright

GERANIUM 'DOPEY'

DESCRIPTION: Leaves dark green, single flowers rose-pink shading to white in center.

REMARKS: Semidwarf and can take abuse if necessary.

SIZE: To 10 inches

TEMPERATURE: 65°–75°F

HUMIDITY: 30 percent

WATERING: Keep evenly moist

LIGHT: Bright

GERANIUM 'FAIRY PRINCESS'

DESCRIPTION: Green leaves with dark markings; bright salmon flowers.

REMARKS: Variegated foliage makes this a popular plant.

SIZE: To 10 inches

TEMPERATURE: 65°–75°F

HUMIDITY: 30 percent

WATERING: Keep evenly moist

LIGHT: Bright

GERANIUM 'FLEURETTE'

DESCRIPTION: Small dark gray-green leaves margined ivory, small orange flowers.

REMARKS: Compact habit and good grower.

SIZE: To 6 inches

TEMPERATURE: 65°–75°F

HUMIDITY: 30 percent

WATERING: Keep evenly moist

LIGHT: Bright

GERANIUM 'GOBLIN'

DESCRIPTION: Dark green foliage, large double flowers bright red.

REMARKS: Compact and very vigorous. Good for beginners.

SIZE: To 6 inches

TEMPERATURE: 65°–75°F

HUMIDITY: 30 percent

WATERING: Keep evenly moist

LIGHT: Bright

GERANIUM 'MEROPE'

DESCRIPTION: Small black-green leaves with black zone, pink flowers; slow growing.

REMARKS: Well known and loved; dark foliage makes nice foil for pink flowers.

SIZE: To 4 inches

TEMPERATURE: 65°–75°F

HUMIDITY: 30 percent

WATERING: Keep evenly moist

LIGHT: Bright

GERANIUM 'METEOR'

DESCRIPTION: Dark black zoned scalloped leaves, double, blood red flowers.

REMARKS: Blooms profusely and makes a handsome pot plant.

SIZE: To 6 inches

TEMPERATURE: 65°–75°F

HUMIDITY: 30 percent

WATERING: Keep evenly moist

LIGHT: Bright

GERANIUM 'PIGMY'

DESCRIPTION: Light green scalloped leaves; free blooming with flat double flowers, vivid red.

REMARKS: Compact growth; excellent grower.

SIZE: To 4 inches

TEMPERATURE: 65°–75°F

HUMIDITY: 30 percent

WATERING: Keep evenly moist

LIGHT: Bright

GERANIUM 'RED COMET'

DESCRIPTION: Butterfly zoned foliage; single flowers with bright red narrow petals with white eye.

REMARKS: Beautiful flowers and foliage.

SIZE: To 6 inches

TEMPERATURE: 65°–75°F

HUMIDITY: 30 percent

WATERING: Keep evenly moist

LIGHT: Bright

GERANIUM 'RUFFLES'

DESCRIPTION: Dark olive to blackish-green leaves; flowers salmon with some ruffled petals.

SIZE: To 4 inches

TEMPERATURE: 65°–75°F

HUMIDITY: 30 percent

WATERING: Keep evenly moist

REMARKS: Stays small, good color.

LIGHT: Bright

GERANIUM 'SALMON COMET'

DESCRIPTION: Narrow-petaled single salmon flowers; tiny leaves marked with dark ring.

SIZE: To 6 inches

TEMPERATURE: 65°–75°F

HUMIDITY: 30 percent

WATERING: Keep evenly moist

REMARKS: Stays small, good color.

LIGHT: Bright

GONGORA ARMENIACA

DESCRIPTION: Broad evergreen leaves, apricot flowers on drooping greenish-purple scape.

SIZE: To 14 inches (pendant)

TEMPERATURE: 72°–80°F

HUMIDITY: 30–40 percent

WATERING: Dry out between waterings

REMARKS: Good hanging orchid; bears dozens of flowers in fall.

LIGHT: Bright

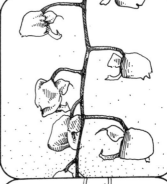

GONGORA GALEATA

DESCRIPTION: Broad evergreen leaves, drooping scapes of pale tawny yellow flowers with brownish-red lip.

SIZE: To 14 inches (pendant)

TEMPERATURE: 72°–80°F

HUMIDITY: 30–40 percent

WATERING: Dry out between waterings

REMARKS: Good hanging orchid; bears many flowers on pendant scapes.

LIGHT: Bright

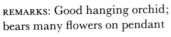

GOODYERA PUBESCENS (rattlesnake plant)

DESCRIPTION: Dark velvety green leaves marked with a network of silvery-white veins; small greenish-white flowers.

SIZE: To 8 inches

TEMPERATURE: 75°–85°F

HUMIDITY: 50 percent

WATERING: Keep evenly moist

REMARKS: One of the foliage orchids; exquisite leaves. Can be difficult.

LIGHT: Shade

GUZMANIA BERTERONIANA

DESCRIPTION: Apple green foliage; rosette growth; orange bracts and yellow flowers.

SIZE: To 18 inches

TEMPERATURE: 60°–75°F

HUMIDITY: 40–50 percent

REMARKS: Bracts stay colorful for four months.

WATERING: Keep evenly moist

LIGHT: Sun

GUZMANIA LINGULATA

DESCRIPTION: Leaves yellow-green; flowers orange-red, white.

SIZE: To 14 inches

TEMPERATURE: 60°–75°F

HUMIDITY: 40–50 percent

REMARKS: One of the best guzmanias; easy to grow.

WATERING: Keep evenly moist

LIGHT: Sun

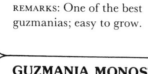

GUZMANIA MONOSTACHIA

DESCRIPTION: Rosette growth, apple green leaves; red, brown and white flower crown.

SIZE: To 20 inches

TEMPERATURE: 60°–75°F

HUMIDITY: 40–50 percent

REMARKS: Great color; blooms in fall. Easy to grow.

WATERING: Keep evenly moist

LIGHT: Sun

GYMNOCALYCIUM BRUCHII

DESCRIPTION: Tiny miniature cactus with 1-inch pale pink flowers.

SIZE: To 4 inches

TEMPERATURE: 72°–80°F

HUMIDITY: 30 percent

REMARKS: Use equal parts sand and soil for potting.

WATERING: Dry out between waterings

LIGHT: Sun

GYMNOCALYCIUM MIHANOVICHI (chin cactus)

DESCRIPTION: Globular shaped, grayish-green with spines; flowers usually pink.

SIZE: To 2 inches

TEMPERATURE: 72°–80°F

HUMIDITY: 30 percent

REMARKS: Use equal parts sand and soil for potting.

WATERING: Dry out between waterings

LIGHT: Sun

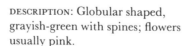

GYMNOCALYCIUM QUEHLIANIUM

DESCRIPTION: Globular red-green body, white flowers with rose center.

REMARKS: Unusual plant; easy to grow.

SIZE: To 6 inches

TEMPERATURE: 72°–80°F

HUMIDITY: 30 percent

WATERING: Dry out between waterings

LIGHT: Sun

GYMNOCALYCIUM SCHICKENDANTZII

DESCRIPTION: Leaves reddish-green; flowers white to pink to yellow.

REMARKS: Grows slowly; impossible to kill.

SIZE: To 4 inches

TEMPERATURE: 72°–80°F

HUMIDITY: 30 percent

WATERING: Dry out between waterings

LIGHT: Sun

HAWORTHIA ATTENUATA

DESCRIPTION: Dark green rosette; short tricornered leaves.

REMARKS: Good for dish gardens; easy, attractive plant to grow.

SIZE: To 6 inches

TEMPERATURE: 72°–80°F

HUMIDITY: 30 percent

WATERING: Dry out between waterings

LIGHT: Sun

HAWORTHIA FASCIATA

DESCRIPTION: Zebra-striped rosette of leaves.

REMARKS: Handsome variegated leaves; very popular.

SIZE: To 4 inches

TEMPERATURE: 72°–80°F

HUMIDITY: 30 percent

WATERING: Dry out between waterings

LIGHT: Sun

HAWORTHIA MARGARITIFERA

DESCRIPTION: Slender tapering deep green leaves; small white flowers in racemes.

REMARKS: A very pretty plant that needs little care.

SIZE: To 6 inches

TEMPERATURE: 72°–80°F

HUMIDITY: 30 percent

WATERING: Dry out between waterings

LIGHT: Sun

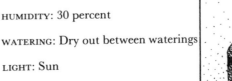

HAWORTHIA TESSELLATA

DESCRIPTION: Tricornered tapering leaves, dark green with pale green lines; reverse reddish.

REMARKS: Oddity looking like carved stone; rest in winter with little water.

SIZE: To 4 inches

TEMPERATURE: 72°–80°F

HUMIDITY: 30 percent

WATERING: Dry out between waterings

LIGHT: Sun

HAWORTHIA TRUNCATA

DESCRIPTION: Oval leaves arranged in two rows; dark greenish-brown.

REMARKS: Not usually grown but worth the search. Unusual.

SIZE: To 6 inches

TEMPERATURE: 72°–80°F

HUMIDITY: 30 percent

WATERING: Dry out between waterings

LIGHT: Sun

HAWORTHIA VICOSA

DESCRIPTION: Elongated rosette of overlapping leaves, dull green and rough; surface concave.

REMARKS: Not spectacular but easy to grow; stays small.

SIZE: To 8 inches

TEMPERATURE: 72°–80°F

HUMIDITY: 30 percent

WATERING: Dry out between waterings

LIGHT: Sun

HEDERA HELIX 'BUTTERCUP' (ivy)

DESCRIPTION: Climbing vine with leaves five-lobed, glossy forest green with creamy veins.

REMARKS: Mist foliage frequently; trim plants occasionally to keep them groomed.

SIZE: To 12 inches

TEMPERATURE: 55°–65°F

HUMIDITY: 30 percent

WATERING: Keep evenly moist

LIGHT: Shade

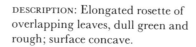

HEDERA HELIX 'CALIFORNIA GOLD'

DESCRIPTION: Rather rounded leaves, light green marbled with yellow.

REMARKS: Grown for its variegated foliage.

SIZE: To 12 inches (pendant)

TEMPERATURE: 55°–65°F

HUMIDITY: 30 percent

WATERING: Keep evenly moist

LIGHT: Shade

HEDERA HELIX 'CURLILOCKS'

DESCRIPTION: Young growths sprouting from every axil of the crested leaves; densely bushy.

REMARKS: Tiny leaves make this a desirable plant.

SIZE: To 12 inches (pendant)

TEMPERATURE: 55°–65°F

HUMIDITY: 30 percent

WATERING: Keep evenly moist

LIGHT: Shade

HEDERA HELIX 'GLACIER'

DESCRIPTION: Variegated, triangular, leathery leaves of several shades of green.

REMARKS: Robust type; good trailer for basket growing.

SIZE: To 20 inches (pendant)

TEMPERATURE: 55°–65°F

HUMIDITY: 30 percent

WATERING: Keep evenly moist

LIGHT: Shade

HEDERA HELIX 'NEEDLEPOINT'

DESCRIPTION: Tiny elongate leaves, usually slender, three-lobed, arranged in ranks facing one side.

REMARKS: Good robust trailer for basket growing; trim and groom plant occasionally.

SIZE: To 14 inches

TEMPERATURE: 55°–65°F

HUMIDITY: 30 percent

WATERING: Keep evenly moist

LIGHT: Shade

HEDERA HELIX 'PIXIE'

DESCRIPTION: Compact, densely shingled small very leathery leaves deeply lobed.

REMARKS: One of the smallest-leaved ivies; popular and easier to grow than most ivies.

SIZE: To 10 inches

TEMPERATURE: 55°–65°F

HUMIDITY: 30 percent

WATERING: Keep evenly moist

LIGHT: Shade

HEPATICA ACUTILOBA

DESCRIPTION: Oval leaves and small rose-colored flowers.

REMARKS: Wildflower; difficult for pot culture but can succeed with care.

SIZE: To 8 inches

TEMPERATURE: 55°–75°F

HUMIDITY: 30 percent

WATERING: Keep evenly moist

LIGHT: Bright

HUMATA TYERMANNII (bear's foot fern)

DESCRIPTION: Creeping light brown rhizome covered with silvery-white scales, leathery fronds.

SIZE: To 8 inches

TEMPERATURE: 72°–80°F

HUMIDITY: 30 percent

REMARKS: Excellent small fern for indoors; don't overwater.

WATERING: Keep evenly moist

LIGHT: Bright

HYACINTHUS AZUREUS

DESCRIPTION: Grasslike leaves and handsome clusters of blue flowers.

SIZE: To 10 inches

TEMPERATURE: 60°–70°F

HUMIDITY: 20–30 percent

REMARKS: Start four corms in an 8-inch pot of soil in fall. Water sparingly until growth starts.

WATERING: Keep evenly moist

LIGHT: Bright

HYACINTHUS CAERULEA

DESCRIPTION: Grasslike leaves and clusters of deep blue flowers.

SIZE: To 10 inches

TEMPERATURE: 60°–70°F

HUMIDITY: 20–30 percent

REMARKS: Start four corms in 8-inch pot of soil in fall. Water sparingly until growth starts.

WATERING: Keep evenly moist

LIGHT: Bright

HYPOCYRTA NUMMULARIA (goldfish plant)

DESCRIPTION: Small shiny dark green leaves and orange flowers shaped like goldfish.

SIZE: To 14 inches

TEMPERATURE: 70°–80°F

HUMIDITY: 30 percent

REMARKS: Sprawling habit; easily grown plant.

WATERING: Keep evenly moist

LIGHT: Sun

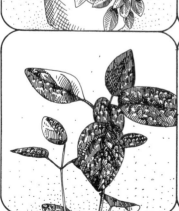

HYPOESTES 'PINK BROCADE'

DESCRIPTION: Downy small green leaves splashed with deep pink; lilac tubular flowers.

SIZE: To 12 inches

TEMPERATURE: 72°–80°F

HUMIDITY: 30 percent

REMARKS: Good plant that does well indoors.

WATERING: Keep evenly moist

LIGHT: Bright

HYPOESTES SANGUINELATA (polka-dot plant)

DESCRIPTION: Pretty oval leaves marked with lavender spots.

REMARKS: Popular; don't allow soil to get too wet.

SIZE: To 12 inches

TEMPERATURE: 72°–80°F

HUMIDITY: 30 percent

WATERING: Keep evenly moist

LIGHT: Bright

IMPATIENS 'HOLSTII'

DESCRIPTION: Succulent branches only 6 inches high; flowers orange.

REMARKS: Lovely; needs some pampering—good light, regular watering.

SIZE: To 18 inches

TEMPERATURE: 65°–80°F

HUMIDITY: 30 percent

WATERING: Keep quite moist

LIGHT: Bright

IMPATIENS 'ORANGE BABY'

DESCRIPTION: Creeping succulent branching 6 inches high; small leaves, deep orange flowers.

REMARKS: Grown for the handsome orange flowers; excellent seasonal plant.

SIZE: To 12 inches

TEMPERATURE: 65°–80°F

HUMIDITY: 30 percent

WATERING: Keep quite moist

LIGHT: Bright

IMPATIENS REPENS

DESCRIPTION: Fleshy red branches, small kidney-shaped leaves, golden-yellow hooded flowers.

REMARKS: Grown for the handsome flowers; excellent seasonal plant.

SIZE: To 14 inches

TEMPERATURE: 65°–80°F

HUMIDITY: 30 percent

WATERING: Keep quite moist

LIGHT: Bright

KAEMPFERIA ROSCOEANA (peacock plant)

DESCRIPTION: Bronzy-chocolate iridescently veined and zoned pale green leaves, pale purple flowers.

REMARKS: After blooming and in late fall store in pot in dark place for a few months. Repot in fresh soil and put at window.

SIZE: To 10 inches

TEMPERATURE: 72°–80°F

HUMIDITY: 30 percent

WATERING: Keep evenly moist

LIGHT: Bright

KALANCHOE TOMENTOSA (panda plant)

DESCRIPTION: Tapered white felt leaves covered with brown dots.

SIZE: To 14 inches

TEMPERATURE: 70°–80°F

HUMIDITY: 30 percent

REMARKS: Handsome succulent; don't overwater, and keep water off leaves.

WATERING: Dry out between waterings

LIGHT: Bright

KALANCHOE 'TOM THUMB'

DESCRIPTION: Green succulent leaves and scarlet-red flowers.

SIZE: To 10 inches

TEMPERATURE: 70°–80°F

HUMIDITY: 30 percent

REMARKS: Cut back to 4 inches in February and you will have a second crop of flowers in April.

WATERING: Dry out between waterings

LIGHT: Bright

KEFERSTIENIA TOLIMENSIS

DESCRIPTION: Tiny grassy leaves, handsome multicolored flowers in abundance.

SIZE: To 2 inches

TEMPERATURE: 75°–85°F

HUMIDITY: 40 percent

REMARKS: Blooms over a long period of time; likes good air circulation.

WATERING: Keep evenly moist

LIGHT: Bright

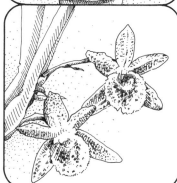

KLEINIA PENDULA

DESCRIPTION: Sugar-frosted gray-green leaves, orange flowers.

SIZE: To 6 inches

TEMPERATURE: 65°–75°F

HUMIDITY: 20–30 percent

REMARKS: A delightful small succulent; use in dish gardens for novel effect.

WATERING: Dry out between waterings

LIGHT: Bright

KLEINIA REPENS

DESCRIPTION: Fleshy nearly cylindrical leaves of gray-blue; yellow flowers.

SIZE: To 4 inches

TEMPERATURE: 65°–75°F

HUMIDITY: 20–30 percent

WATERING: Dry out between waterings

REMARKS: A delightful small succulent; use in dish gardens.

LIGHT: Bright

LITHOPS BELLA (living stones)

DESCRIPTION: Small succulent plant with two thick leaves, brownish-yellow with darker markings. White flowers.

REMARKS: Put a ½-inch bed of gravel on top of soil; do not overwater.

SIZE: To 1 inch

TEMPERATURE: 75°–85°F

HUMIDITY: 20 percent

WATERING: Keep dry

LIGHT: Sun

LITHOPS TERRICOLOR

DESCRIPTION: Grayish stone-shaped leaves dotted with red; yellow flowers.

REMARKS: Put a ½-inch bed of gravel on top of soil; do not overwater.

SIZE: To 1 inch

TEMPERATURE: 75°–85°F

HUMIDITY: 20 percent

WATERING: Keep dry

LIGHT: Sun

LITHOPS TRIEBNERI

DESCRIPTION: Beige-gray split leaves, yellow flowers.

REMARKS: Put a ½-inch bed of gravel on top of soil; do not overwater.

SIZE: To 2 inches

TEMPERATURE: 75°–85°F

HUMIDITY: 20 percent

WATERING: Keep dry

LIGHT: Sun

LOBIVIA AUREA

DESCRIPTION: Small pale green globe; flowers carmine with bluish sheen.

REMARKS: Large flowers for size of plant; grow in equal parts sand and soil.

SIZE: To 3 inches

TEMPERATURE: 70°–80°F

HUMIDITY: 20 percent

WATERING: Dry out between waterings

LIGHT: Sun

LOBIVIA BACKEBERGII

DESCRIPTION: Small globe, ribbed; handsome red flowers.

REMARKS: Large flowers for size of plant; grow in equal parts sand and soil.

SIZE: To 4 inches

TEMPERATURE: 70°–80°F

HUMIDITY: 20 percent

WATERING: Dry out between waterings

LIGHT: Sun

LOBIVIA LONGISPINA

DESCRIPTION: Globular plant, ribbed with brown to gray central spines and white flowers.

REMARKS: Rest slightly with less water in winter.

SIZE: To 6 inches

TEMPERATURE: 70°–80°F

HUMIDITY: 20 percent

WATERING: Dry out between waterings

LIGHT: Sun

LOBIVIA PENTLANDII

DESCRIPTION: Globular plant, somewhat branching, glaucous green with ribs; rose-colored flowers.

REMARKS: Rest slightly with less water in winter.

SIZE: To 8 inches

TEMPERATURE: 70°–80°F

HUMIDITY: 20 percent

WATERING: Dry out between waterings

LIGHT: Sun

LOBIVIA ROSSII

DESCRIPTION: Small globe shape, very ribbed; funnel-shaped red flowers.

REMARKS: Rest slightly with less water in winter.

SIZE: To 6 inches

TEMPERATURE: 70°–80°F

HUMIDITY: 20 percent

WATERING: Dry out between waterings

LIGHT: Sun

LOCKHARTIA ACUTA

DESCRIPTION: Small bright green leaves; flowers solitary, yellow spotted red.

REMARKS: Grow on tree fern slab; blooms on and off throughout the year.

SIZE: To 10 inches

TEMPERATURE: 72°–80°F

HUMIDITY: 30–40 percent

WATERING: Keep wet

LIGHT: Sun

LOCKHARTIA LUNIFERA

DESCRIPTION: Orchid with triangular pendant leaves and tiny golden-yellow flowers.

REMARKS: Grow on tree fern slab; blooms on and off throughout the year.

SIZE: To 10 inches

TEMPERATURE: 72°–80°F

HUMIDITY: 30–40 percent

WATERING: Keep wet

LIGHT: Sun

MALPIGHIA COCCIGERA (miniature holly)

DESCRIPTION: Bushy evergreen shrub with tiny glossy dark green leaves; small pink flowers, red fruit.

REMARKS: Stays bright and pretty for months.

SIZE: To 18 inches

TEMPERATURE: 65°–75°F

HUMIDITY: 30 percent

WATERING: Keep evenly moist

LIGHT: Bright

MAMMILLARIA BOCASANA (pincushion cactus)

DESCRIPTION: Clustering growth, hooked central spine covered with white hair, small yellow flowers.

REMARKS: Easily grown; give winter rest with scanty waterings.

SIZE: To 10 inches

TEMPERATURE: 75°–85°F

HUMIDITY: 20 percent

WATERING: Dry out between waterings

LIGHT: Sun

MAMMILLARIA HAHNIANA (old lady cactus)

DESCRIPTION: Attractive globe, rich green with long curly snowy white bristles; flowers violet-red.

REMARKS: Winter flowers; very desirable.

SIZE: To 10 inches

TEMPERATURE: 75°–85°F

HUMIDITY: 20 percent

WATERING: Dry out between waterings

LIGHT: Sun

MAMMILLARIA LEWISIANA

DESCRIPTION: A flattened deep green globe and a curving black-brown central spine; yellow flowers.

REMARKS: Give winter rest with scanty waterings.

SIZE: To 8 inches

TEMPERATURE: 75°–85°F

HUMIDITY: 20 percent

WATERING: Dry out between waterings

LIGHT: Sun

MAMMILLARIA TEGELBERGIANA

DESCRIPTION: Perfect globe with stout central spines tipped brown-black; rose flowers.

REMARKS: Give winter rest with scanty waterings.

SIZE: To 6 inches

TEMPERATURE: 75°–85°F

HUMIDITY: 20 percent

WATERING: Dry out between waterings

LIGHT: Sun

MAMMILLARIA ZEILMANNIANA

DESCRIPTION: Glossy green globe with knobs and reddish spines; violet flowers.

REMARKS: Give winter rest with scanty waterings.

SIZE: To 8 inches

TEMPERATURE: 75°–85°F

HUMIDITY: 20 percent

WATERING: Dry out between waterings

LIGHT: Sun

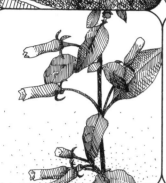

MANETTIA BICOLOR (Mexican firecracker)

DESCRIPTION: Twining plant with threadlike stems and small yellow waxy flowers.

REMARKS: Thrives when potbound and requires an airy location.

SIZE: To 16 inches

TEMPERATURE: 55°–75°F

HUMIDITY: 30 percent

WATERING: Dry out between waterings

LIGHT: Sun

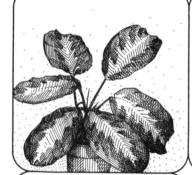

MARANTA BICOLOR

DESCRIPTION: Light green leaves with brown spots, purple beneath.

REMARKS: Pretty plant but somewhat temperamental.

SIZE: To 16 inches

TEMPERATURE: 70°–80°F

HUMIDITY: 30 percent

WATERING: Keep evenly moist

LIGHT: Shade

MARANTA MASSANGEANA (prayer plant)

DESCRIPTION: Bluish-green leaves with a silver feather design, striped pink and reddish-brown.

REMARKS: In late fall cut back stems somewhat to encourage new growth.

SIZE: To 14inches

TEMPERATURE: 70°–80°F

HUMIDITY: 30 percent

WATERING: Keep evenly moist

LIGHT: Shade

MARANTA REPENS

DESCRIPTION: Leaves similar to M. massangeana, but smaller.

REMARKS: Very pretty plant; grown for exquisite foliage.

SIZE: To 12 inches

TEMPERATURE: 70°–80°F

HUMIDITY: 30 percent

WATERING: Keep evenly moist

LIGHT: Shade

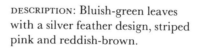

MASDEVALLIA BELLA

DESCRIPTION: Spatula-shaped leaves, thick and leathery; triangular pale yellow flowers.

REMARKS: Give cool temperature to encourage bloom.

SIZE: To 4 inches

TEMPERATURE: 55°–70°F

HUMIDITY: 30 percent

WATERING: Keep evenly moist

LIGHT: Bright

MASDEVALLIA CAUDATA

DESCRIPTION: Leathery grasslike leaves and whitish-yellow triangular flowers.

REMARKS: Give cool temperature to encourage bloom.

SIZE: To 6 inches

TEMPERATURE: 55°–70°F

HUMIDITY: 30 percent

WATERING: Keep evenly moist

LIGHT: Bright

MASDEVALLIA COCCINEA (kite orchid)

DESCRIPTION: Spatula-shaped leaves, wiry stems with brilliant red flowers.

REMARKS: Outstanding, and flowers last for weeks in fall.

SIZE: To 10 inches

TEMPERATURE: 55°–70°F

HUMIDITY: 30 percent

WATERING: Keep evenly moist

LIGHT: Bright

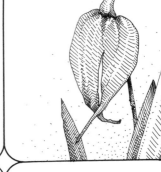

MASDEVALLIA HORRIDA

DESCRIPTION: Tufted leaves, greenish and bristly, hairy inside; red cupped flowers with yellow tails.

REMARKS: An absolute charmer despite its name.

SIZE: To 3 inches

TEMPERATURE: 55°–70°F

HUMIDITY: 30 percent

WATERING: Keep evenly moist

LIGHT: Bright

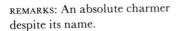

MASDEVALLIA TOVARENSIS

DESCRIPTION: Elliptical long stalked leaves and wiry stems with white flowers.

REMARKS: Easy to grow indoors; needs cool temperature to prosper.

SIZE: To 8 inches

TEMPERATURE: 55°–70°F

HUMIDITY: 30 percent

WATERING: Keep evenly moist

LIGHT: Bright

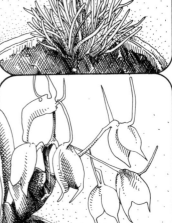

MICROLEPIA SETOSA

DESCRIPTION: Fern with lacy, hairy fronds borne on slender 1-foot stalks.

REMARKS: Handsome small fern for indoors.

SIZE: To 6 inches

TEMPERATURE: 72°–80°F

HUMIDITY: 30 percent

WATERING: Keep wet

LIGHT: Shade

MUEHLENBECKIA COMPLEXA (wireplant)

DESCRIPTION: Twining, threadlike, purplish-brown wiry stems, tiny round green leaves, white flowers.

REMARKS: A fine plant for basket growing.

SIZE: To 10 inches

TEMPERATURE: 60°–75°F

HUMIDITY: 30 percent

WATERING: Keep barely moist

LIGHT: Sun

MUSCARI ARMENIACUM (grape hyacinth)

DESCRIPTION: Narrow leaves and delicate nodding urn-shaped blue flowers.

REMARKS: Always makes a charming pot plant; start four corms in an 8-inch pot of soil in fall.

SIZE: To 8 inches

TEMPERATURE: 60°–80°F

HUMIDITY: 30 percent

WATERING: Keep evenly moist

LIGHT: Bright

MUSCARI BOTRYOIDES

DESCRIPTION: Dark green leaves, blue flowers lined white.

REMARKS: Always makes a charming pot plant; start four corms in an 8-inch pot of soil in fall.

SIZE: To 6 inches

TEMPERATURE: 60°–80°F

HUMIDITY: 30 percent

WATERING: Keep evenly moist

LIGHT: Bright

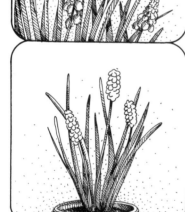

MUSCARI COMOSUM

DESCRIPTION: Dark green strap-shaped leaves, purple-blue flowers.

REMARKS: Always makes a charming pot plant; start four corms in an 8-inch pot of soil in fall.

SIZE: To 6 inches

TEMPERATURE: 60°–80°F

HUMIDITY: 30 percent

WATERING: Keep evenly moist

LIGHT: Bright

NARCISSUS BULBOCODIUM

DESCRIPTION: Yellow hoop-petticoat daffodil; flowers rich golden color.

SIZE: To 10 inches

TEMPERATURE: 60°–80°F

HUMIDITY: 30 percent

REMARKS: Delightful indoor bulbous plant; good for one season. Grow in gravel.

WATERING: Keep evenly moist

LIGHT: Sun (after leaves are up)

NARCISSUS CAMPERNELLI 'ORANGE QUEEN'

DESCRIPTION: Fragrant flowers of apricot orange clustered four on a stem.

SIZE: To 10 inches

TEMPERATURE: 60°–80°F

HUMIDITY: 30 percent

REMARKS: Try in pots; sometimes blooms indoors.

WATERING: Keep evenly moist

LIGHT: Sun (after leaves are up)

NARCISSUS CYCLAMINEUS

DESCRIPTION: Downward pointed trumpet of vibrant yellow, frilled at edge.

SIZE: To 10 inches

TEMPERATURE: 60°–80°F

HUMIDITY: 30 percent

REMARKS: One of the best, with delightful flowers.

WATERING: Keep evenly moist

LIGHT: Sun (after leaves are up)

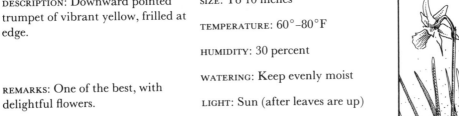

NARCISSUS JUNCIFOLIUS

DESCRIPTION: Small graceful flowers of rich yellow with a dainty flat crown.

SIZE: To 10 inches

TEMPERATURE: 60°–80°F

HUMIDITY: 30 percent

REMARKS: Small flowers; handsome seasonal color.

WATERING: Keep evenly moist

LIGHT: Sun (after leaves are up)

NARCISSUS NANUS

DESCRIPTION: Smallest trumpet daffodil; flowers are bright buttercup yellow.

SIZE: To 5 inches

TEMPERATURE: 60°–80°F

HUMIDITY: 30 percent

REMARKS: Grow in pots indoors for splendid color.

WATERING: Keep evenly moist

LIGHT: Sun (after leaves are up)

NARCISSUS TRIANDUS ALBUS

DESCRIPTION: Angel's tear daffodil; clusters of cream-white flowers.

SIZE: To 10 inches

TEMPERATURE: 60°–80°F

HUMIDITY: 30 percent

REMARKS: Large flowers; handsome seasonal color.

WATERING: Keep evenly moist

LIGHT: Sun (after leaves come up)

NEPETA CATARITICA (catnip)

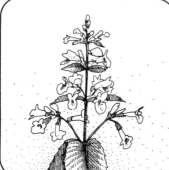

DESCRIPTION: Oval gray leaves, hairy; pale purple flowers.

SIZE: To 4 inches

TEMPERATURE: 55°–75°F

HUMIDITY: 30 percent

REMARKS: Makes a nice basket plant or use as ground cover for plants in big pots.

WATERING: Keep evenly moist

LIGHT: Shade

NEPETA HEDERACEA

DESCRIPTION: Creeping perennial, mat-forming; blue flowers. Small fresh green leaves.

SIZE: To 4 inches

TEMPERATURE: 55°–75°F

HUMIDITY: 30 percent

REMARKS: Makes a nice basket plant or use as ground cover for plants in big pots.

WATERING: Keep evenly moist

LIGHT: Shade

NOTOCACTUS HASELBERGII

DESCRIPTION: Globular growth covered with soft white spines; bright red blossoms.

SIZE: To 8 inches

TEMPERATURE: 70°–80°F

HUMIDITY: 30 percent

REMARKS: Fine cactus for indoors; large flowers.

WATERING: Dry out between waterings

LIGHT: Sun

NOTOCACTUS LENINGHAUSII

DESCRIPTION: Cylindrical column covered with soft golden hair; yellow flowers.

SIZE: To 8 inches

TEMPERATURE: 70°–80°F

HUMIDITY: 30 percent

REMARKS: Fine cactus for indoors; large flowers.

WATERING: Dry out between waterings

LIGHT: Sun

NOTOCACTUS OTTONIS

DESCRIPTION: Clustering globular plant with bristly red-brown spines; yellow flowers.

REMARKS: True miniature and a delightful plant. Rest with scanty watering in winter.

SIZE: To 2 inches

TEMPERATURE: 70°–80°F

HUMIDITY: 30 percent

WATERING: Dry out between waterings

LIGHT: Sun

NOTOCACTUS RUTILANS

DESCRIPTION: Dark green globe with knobs and brownish central spine; bright pink flowers.

REMARKS: Rest somewhat in winter with scanty watering.

SIZE: To 6 inches

TEMPERATURE: 70°–80°F

HUMIDITY: 30 percent

WATERING: Dry out between waterings

LIGHT: Sun

NOTOCACTUS SCOPA

DESCRIPTION: Globular, ribbed, covered with soft white spines; yellow flowers.

REMARKS: Rest somewhat in winter with scanty watering.

SIZE: To 8 inches

TEMPERATURE: 70°–80°F

HUMIDITY: 30 percent

WATERING: Dry out between waterings

LIGHT: Sun

NOTOCACTUS SUBMAMMULOSUS (lemon ball)

DESCRIPTION: Small shining green globe with rows of knobs; yellow flowers.

REMARKS: Rest somewhat in winter with scanty waterings.

SIZE: To 3 inches

TEMPERATURE: 75°–85°F

HUMIDITY: 20 percent

WATERING: Dry out between waterings

LIGHT: Sun

ODONTOGLOSSUM PULCHELLUM

DESCRIPTION: Many small leaves tipped with one or two large leaves; tiny white scented flowers.

REMARKS: A miniature orchid grown for fragrance.

SIZE: To 6 inches

TEMPERATURE: 65°–75°F

HUMIDITY: 30 percent

WATERING: Keep evenly moist

LIGHT: Bright

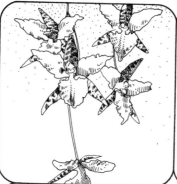

ODONTOGLOSSUM ROSSII

DESCRIPTION: Pseudobulbs sheathed with small leaves; white or rose small flowers.

SIZE: To 6 inches

TEMPERATURE: 65°–75°F

HUMIDITY: 30 percent

WATERING: Keep evenly moist

REMARKS: Another small orchid; easy to grow.

LIGHT: Bright

ONCIDIUM AMPLIATUM

DESCRIPTION: Pseudobulbs tipped by one or two fleshy leaves; spray-type flowers of yellow and red-brown.

SIZE: To 12 inches

TEMPERATURE: 70°–80°F

HUMIDITY: 30–40 percent

WATERING: Keep evenly moist

REMARKS: Good robust orchid; dependable to bloom in spring.

LIGHT: Sun

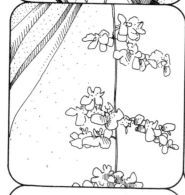

ONCIDIUM CHEIROPHORUM

DESCRIPTION: Six inches high with yellow and chestnut-brown flowers.

SIZE: To 6 inches

TEMPERATURE: 70°–80°F

HUMIDITY: 30–40 percent

WATERING: Keep evenly moist

REMARKS: Has many flowers in late fall; give cool (60°F) winter rest.

LIGHT: Sun

ONCIDIUM POWELLII

DESCRIPTION: Creeping growth habit with 1- to 2-inch leaves; chocolate brown flowers tipped yellow.

SIZE: To 6 inches

TEMPERATURE: 70°–80°F

HUMIDITY: 30–40 percent

WATERING: Keep evenly moist

REMARKS: Has many flowers in late fall; give cool (60°F) winter rest.

LIGHT: Sun

ONCIDIUM PUSILLUM

DESCRIPTION: Small fleshy leaves in fan shape; pale yellow flowers.

SIZE: To 3 inches

TEMPERATURE: 70°–80°F

HUMIDITY: 30–40 percent

WATERING: Keep evenly moist

REMARKS: Nice color in summer; keep warm.

LIGHT: Sun

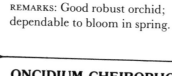

ONCIDIUM TRIQUETRUM

DESCRIPTION: Tufted leaves, greenish flowers bordered white.

SIZE: To 4 inches

TEMPERATURE: 70°–80°F

HUMIDITY: 30–40 percent

WATERING: Keep evenly moist

LIGHT: Sun

REMARKS: A very floriferous small orchid.

OPUNTIA BASILARIS (beaver-pad cactus)

DESCRIPTION: Upright blue-green growths from compact pads; pink to carmine flowers.

SIZE: To 16 inches

TEMPERATURE: 72°–80°F

HUMIDITY: 30 percent

WATERING: Dry out between waterings

LIGHT: Sun

REMARKS: Rarely blooms indoors but has a nice branching habit.

OPUNTIA ERINACEA (grizzly bear)

DESCRIPTION: Thick flattened leaves covered with spines; yellow or pink flowers.

SIZE: To 12 inches

TEMPERATURE: 72°–80°F

HUMIDITY: 30 percent

WATERING: Dry out between waterings

LIGHT: Sun

REMARKS: Move to cooler place in winter, and give less water.

OPUNTIA MICRODASYS (bunny ears)

DESCRIPTION: Oblong spineless pads covered by tufts of golden bristles

SIZE: To 24 inches

TEMPERATURE: 72°–80°F

HUMIDITY: 30 percent

WATERING: Dry out between waterings

LIGHT: Sun

REMARKS: Most popular but not a strong plant.

ORNITHOCEPHALUS GRANDIFLORUS

DESCRIPTION: Tufted growth and fleshy wedge-shaped leaves; small whitish-green flowers.

SIZE: To 6 inches

TEMPERATURE: 72°–80°F

HUMIDITY: 30–40 percent

WATERING: Keep evenly moist

LIGHT: Sun

REMARKS: Handsome small orchid and does bloom indoors; grow in fir bark.

ORTHOPHYTUM NAVIOIDES

DESCRIPTION: Leaves green, flowers white.

REMARKS: Stubborn bromeliad that rarely blooms indoors but has unusual growth habit.

SIZE: To 8 inches

TEMPERATURE: 70°–80°F

HUMIDITY: 30 percent

WATERING: Dry out between waterings

LIGHT: Sun

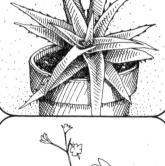

ORTHOPHYTUM SAXICOLA

DESCRIPTION: Leaves green, flowers white.

REMARKS: Easier to grow than the above.

SIZE: To 10 inches

TEMPERATURE: 70°–80°F

HUMIDITY: 30 percent

WATERING: Dry out between waterings

LIGHT: Sun

OXALIS BOWIEI

DESCRIPTION: Leaves metallic green, pink to purple flowers.

REMARKS: Most popular and easily grown.

SIZE: To 10 inches

TEMPERATURE: 70°–80°F

HUMIDITY: 30 percent

WATERING: Dry out between waterings

LIGHT: Sun

OXALIS CARNOSA

DESCRIPTION: Small succulent leaves with single yellow flowers; tuberous.

REMARKS: Grows like a weed and blooms, too.

SIZE: To 6 inches

TEMPERATURE: 65°–75°F

HUMIDITY: 30 percent

WATERING: Keep wet

LIGHT: Sun

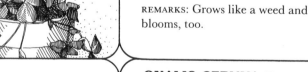

OXALIS CERNUA (Bermuda buttercup)

DESCRIPTION: Double buttercup, tuberous. Double yellow flowers marked brown.

REMARKS: Rest in winter; leave corms in pots.

SIZE: To 6 inches

TEMPERATURE: 65°–75°F

HUMIDITY: 30 percent

WATERING: Keep wet

LIGHT: Sun

OXALIS HEDYSAROIDES (firefern)

DESCRIPTION: Fibrous-rooted, bright yellow flowers, fernlike wine-red foliage.

SIZE: To 6 inches

TEMPERATURE: 65°–75°F

HUMIDITY: 30 percent

WATERING: Keep wet

LIGHT: Sun

REMARKS: Rest in winter; leave corms in pots.

OXALIS HERRERAE

DESCRIPTION: Densely branched woody stem with three tiny fleshy leaflets; small red flowers.

SIZE: To 6 inches

TEMPERATURE: 65°–75°F

HUMIDITY: 30 percent

WATERING: Keep wet

LIGHT: Sun

REMARKS: Rest in winter; leave corms in pots.

OXALIS HIRTA

DESCRIPTION: Tuberous. Feathery foliage, deep violet-purple flowers with yellow throat.

SIZE: To 6 inches

TEMPERATURE: 65°–75°F

HUMIDITY: 30 percent

WATERING: Keep wet

LIGHT: Sun

REMARKS: Rest in winter; leave corms in pots.

OXALIS MELANOSTICHA

DESCRIPTION: Tuberous. Three leaf segments covered with gray hair; yellow flowers.

SIZE: To 6 inches

TEMPERATURE: 65°–75°F

HUMIDITY: 30 percent

WATERING: Keep wet

LIGHT: Sun

REMARKS: Rest in spring and summer.

OXALIS REGNELLII

DESCRIPTION: Tuberous; grasslike leaves, white flowers.

SIZE: To 6 inches

TEMPERATURE: 65°–75°F

HUMIDITY: 30 percent

WATERING: Keep wet

LIGHT: Sun

REMARKS: Grows like a weed and blooms, too.

OXALIS RUBRA

DESCRIPTION: Erect, shrubby, wire stem and thin, fernlike foliage; many small rose flowers.

SIZE: To 6 inches

TEMPERATURE: 65°–75°F

HUMIDITY: 30 percent

WATERING: Keep wet

REMARKS: Rest in winter.

LIGHT: Sun

PARODIA AUREISPINA (tom thumb cactus)

DESCRIPTION: Small globular plant with golden spines, yellow flowers.

SIZE: To 6 inches

TEMPERATURE: 72°–80°F

HUMIDITY: 30 percent

REMARKS: Fine cactus; big flowers for size of plant. Rest with little water in winter.

WATERING: Dry out between waterings

LIGHT: Sun

PARODIA MAASII

DESCRIPTION: Yellowish-green globe with prominent ribs and hooked spines, orange-red flowers.

SIZE: To 4 inches

TEMPERATURE: 72°–80°F

HUMIDITY: 30 percent

REMARKS: Fine cactus; big flowers for size of plant. Rest with little water in winter.

WATERING: Dry out between waterings

LIGHT: Sun

PARODIA MUTABILIS

DESCRIPTION: Globe of olive green; hooked orange spines and golden-yellow flowers.

SIZE: To 3 inches

TEMPERATURE: 72°–80°F

HUMIDITY: 30 percent

REMARKS: One of the best; blooms indoors with good sun. Rest somewhat in winter.

WATERING: Dry out between waterings

LIGHT: Sun

PARODIA SANGUINIFLORA

DESCRIPTION: Small white-spined species, globular with red flowers.

SIZE: To 6 inches

TEMPERATURE: 72°–80°F

HUMIDITY: 30 percent

WATERING: Dry out between waterings

REMARKS: Don't miss this one.

LIGHT: Sun

PELLAEA ROTUNDIFOLIA (button fern)

DESCRIPTION: Fern with creeping rhizome and stems; leaves round when young, later oblong, dark green and waxy.

REMARKS: A fine window fern; mist with water occasionally.

SIZE: To 10 inches

TEMPERATURE: 70°–78°F

HUMIDITY: 30 percent

WATERING: Keep wet

LIGHT: Shade

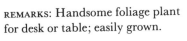

SIZE: To 8 inches

TEMPERATURE: 72°–80°F

HUMIDITY: 30 percent

WATERING: Dry out between waterings

LIGHT: Bright

...ERALD RIPPLE'

SIZE: To 10 inches

TEMPERATURE: 72°–80°F

HUMIDITY: 30 percent

WATERING: Dry out between waterings

LIGHT: Bright

...ATA 'LITTLE FANTASY'

DESCRIPTION: Very small green pointed leaves marked brown.

REMARKS: Handsome foliage plant for desk or table; easily grown.

SIZE: To 6 inches

TEMPERATURE: 72°–80°F

HUMIDITY: 30 percent

WATERING: Dry out between waterings

LIGHT: Bright

PEPEROMIA CAPERATA 'VARIEGATA'

DESCRIPTION: Stiff waxy dark green leaves margined with white.

REMARKS: Handsome foliage plant for desk or table; easily grown.

SIZE: To 10 inches

TEMPERATURE: 72°–80°F

HUMIDITY: 30 percent

WATERING: Dry out between waterings

LIGHT: Bright

PEPEROMIA CLUSIAEFOLIA

DESCRIPTION: Thick fleshy narrow leaves, metallic olive green and red-purple margin, light green beneath.

REMARKS: Grows easily; use for terrariums or dish gardens.

SIZE: To 10 inches

TEMPERATURE: 72°–80°F

HUMIDITY: 30 percent

WATERING: Dry out between waterings

LIGHT: Bright

PEPEROMIA FOSTERI

DESCRIPTION: Thick foliage, forest green with light green markings.

REMARKS: Grows easily; use for terrariums or dish gardens.

SIZE: To 10 inches

TEMPERATURE: 72°–80°F

HUMIDITY: 30 percent

WATERING: Dry out between waterings

LIGHT: Bright

PEPEROMIA GRISEO-ARGENTEA

DESCRIPTION: Bushy rosette with round quilted leaves, silver and purplish-olive.

REMARKS: Outstanding for table or desk accent.

SIZE: To 10 inches

TEMPERATURE: 72°–80°F

HUMIDITY: 30 percent

WATERING: Dry out between waterings

LIGHT: Bright

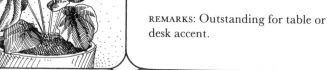

PEPEROMIA GRISEO-ARGENTEA 'BLACKIE'

DESCRIPTION: Thin waxy leaves of metallic olive green to blackish-copper with gray on the reverse side.

REMARKS: Outstanding for table or desk accent.

SIZE: To 10 inches

TEMPERATURE: 72°–80°F

HUMIDITY: 30 percent

WATERING: Dry out between waterings

LIGHT: Bright

PEPEROMIA INCANA

DESCRIPTION: Stiff green leaves, heart-shaped and covered with white hairs.

REMARKS: Good for terrariums or dish gardens.

SIZE: To 10 inches

TEMPERATURE: 72°–80°F

HUMIDITY: 30 percent

WATERING: Dry out between waterings

LIGHT: Bright

PEPEROMIA MARMORATA 'SILVER HEART'

DESCRIPTION: Heart-shaped leaves, green to bluish; ridges marked silver-gray between grass green veins.

REMARKS: Good for terrariums or dish gardens.

SIZE: To 10 inches

TEMPERATURE: 72°–80°F

HUMIDITY: 30 percent

WATERING: Dry out between waterings

LIGHT: Bright

PEPEROMIA METALLICA

DESCRIPTION: Dark reddish stems and waxy copper leaves with silver-green bands.

REMARKS: Good for terrariums or dish gardens.

SIZE: To 10 inches

TEMPERATURE: 72°–80°F

HUMIDITY: 30 percent

WATERING: Dry out between waterings

LIGHT: Bright

PEPEROMIA OBTUSIFOLIA VARIEGATA

DESCRIPTION: Round waxy milky green leaves marked with light green.

REMARKS: One of the best and easy to grow.

SIZE: To 10 inches

TEMPERATURE: 72°–80°F

HUMIDITY: 30 percent

WATERING: Dry out between waterings

LIGHT: Bright

PERPEROMIA OBTUSIFOLIA ALBA MARGINATA 'MINIMA'

DESCRIPTION: Thick fleshy oval leaves variegated with cream and suffused with pale green.

REMARKS: Special variety; exquisite leaves.

SIZE: To 10 inches

TEMPERATURE: 72°–80°F

HUMIDITY: 30 percent

WATERING: Dry out between waterings

LIGHT: Bright

PEPEROMIA ORNATA

DESCRIPTION: Fleshy leaves silky green above with light veins.

REMARKS: Nice for table or desk accent.

SIZE: To 10 inches

TEMPERATURE: 72°–80°F

HUMIDITY: 30 percent

WATERING: Dry out between waterings

LIGHT: Bright

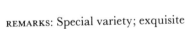

PEPEROMIA RUBELLA

DESCRIPTION: Whorls of tiny obovate leaves, olive green, silver network, crimson beneath.

SIZE: To 10 inches

TEMPERATURE: 72°–80°F

HUMIDITY: 30 percent

WATERING: Dry out between waterings

LIGHT: Bright

REMARKS: Nice for table or desk accent.

PEPEROMIA SANDERSII (watermelon peperomia)

DESCRIPTION: Rosette of concave glossy fresh green leaves, showy bands of silver, white catkins.

SIZE: To 10 inches

TEMPERATURE: 72°–80°F

HUMIDITY: 30 percent

WATERING: Dry out between waterings

LIGHT: Bright

REMARKS: Use anyplace in the home for a green accent.

PEPEROMIA SCANDENS

DESCRIPTION: Fleshy reddish stems and waxy fresh green heart-shaped leaves.

SIZE: To 10 inches

TEMPERATURE: 72°–80°F

HUMIDITY: 30 percent

WATERING: Dry out between waterings

LIGHT: Bright

REMARKS: Use anyplace in the home for a green accent.

PEPEROMIA VERTICILLATA

DESCRIPTION: Hairy stems and small oval leaves, pale green tinted red.

SIZE: To 10 inches

TEMPERATURE: 72°–80°F

HUMIDITY: 30 percent

WATERING: Dry out between waterings

LIGHT: Bright

REMARKS: Use anyplace in the home for a green accent.

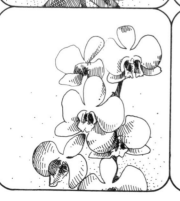

PHALAENOPSIS BUYSSONIANA

DESCRIPTION: Short stems with three or more leathery leaves. Flowers crimson-purple.

SIZE: To 10 inches

TEMPERATURE: 72°–85°F

HUMIDITY: 40 percent

WATERING: Keep evenly moist

LIGHT: Bright

REMARKS: Keep out of direct sun; lovely late summer flowers.

PHALAENOPSIS ESMERALDA

DESCRIPTION: Dark green leaves, 6 inches long; bears delicate pink or rose flowers.

REMARKS: Keep out of direct sun; lovely late summer flowers.

SIZE: To 8 inches

TEMPERATURE: 72°–85°F

HUMIDITY: 40 percent

WATERING: Keep evenly moist

LIGHT: Bright

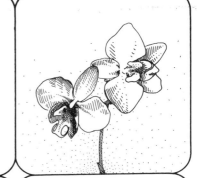

PHALAENOPSIS LUDDEMANNIANA

DESCRIPTION: Leaves 6 to 10 inches long; 2-inch flowers, white, barred amethyst.

REMARKS: Good for fall color; keep out of direct sun.

SIZE: To 10 inches

TEMPERATURE: 72°–85°F

HUMIDITY: 40 percent

WATERING: Keep evenly moist

LIGHT: Bright

PHALAENOPSIS MANNII

DESCRIPTION: Golden-yellow flowers blotched with brown, the lip light yellow fringed purple.

REMARKS: Exotic orchid for that special place; dry out slightly after blooming.

SIZE: To 10 inches

TEMPERATURE: 72°–85°F

HUMIDITY: 40 percent

WATERING: Keep evenly moist

LIGHT: Bright

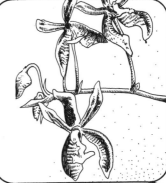

PHALAENOPSIS PARISHII

DESCRIPTION: Two- to four-inch leaves; white flowers spotted purple, fringed lip has yellow-brown center.

REMARKS: Exotic orchid for that special place; dry out slightly after blooming.

SIZE: To 6 inches

TEMPERATURE: 72°–85°F

HUMIDITY: 40 percent

WATERING: Keep evenly moist

LIGHT: Bright

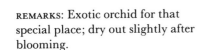

PHALAENOPSIS ROSEA

DESCRIPTION: Leaves about 8 inches long; has tiny white or rose flowers.

REMARKS: Exotic orchid for that special place; dry out slightly after blooming.

SIZE: To 6 inches

TEMPERATURE: 72°–85°F

HUMIDITY: 40 percent

WATERING: Keep evenly moist

LIGHT: Bright

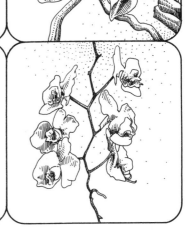

PHILODENDRON MICANS

DESCRIPTION: Small heart-shaped leaves, glittering silky bronze above, reddish beneath.

SIZE: To 12 inches

TEMPERATURE: 72°–80°F

HUMIDITY: 30 percent

WATERING: Dry out between waterings

REMARKS: Nice small philodendron; mist with water frequently.

LIGHT: Bright

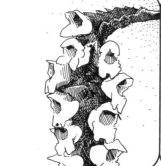

PHOLIDOTA IMBRICATA

DESCRIPTION: Single leaves or pseudobulbs and pendant stems of shell-like yellowish-white flowers.

SIZE: To 10 inches (pendant)

TEMPERATURE: 72°–80°F

HUMIDITY: 30 percent

WATERING: Keep evenly moist

REMARKS: Give some winter sun; good orchid for hanging baskets.

LIGHT: Bright

PHOLIDOTA PALLIDA

DESCRIPTION: Plaited leaves and cupped cream-colored flowers.

SIZE: To 10 inches (pendant)

TEMPERATURE: 72°–80°F

HUMIDITY: 30 percent

WATERING: Keep evenly moist

REMARKS: Give some winter sun; good orchid for hanging baskets.

LIGHT: Bright

PILEA CADIEREI 'MINIMA' (aluminum plant)

DESCRIPTION: Elliptic, pointed, quilted leaves, deep olive green with silver areas.

SIZE: To 12 inches

TEMPERATURE: 70°–80°F

HUMIDITY: 20–30 percent

WATERING: Keep evenly moist

REMARKS: Handsome decorative plant for terrariums or dish gardens.

LIGHT: Bright

PILEA DEPRESSA

DESCRIPTION: Tiny ¼-inch roundish obovate fleshy leaves, light pea green and glossy on thin stems.

SIZE: To 10 inches

TEMPERATURE: 70°–80°F

HUMIDITY: 20–30 percent

WATERING: Keep evenly moist

REMARKS: Handsome decorative plant for terrariums or dish gardens.

LIGHT: Bright

PILEA INVOLUCRATA

DESCRIPTION: Oval, somewhat fleshy leaves deep green; tiny rosy red flowers.

SIZE: To 12 inches

TEMPERATURE: 70°–80°F

HUMIDITY: 20–30 percent

WATERING: Keep evenly moist

LIGHT: Bright

REMARKS: Good ground cover for large potted plants.

PILEA MICROPHYLLA (artillery plant)

DESCRIPTION: Thick fleshy stems with tiny succulent green leaves, clusters of white flowers.

SIZE: To 6 inches

TEMPERATURE: 70°–80°F

HUMIDITY: 20–30 percent

WATERING: Keep evenly moist

LIGHT: Bright

REMARKS: Forms mat of leaves; unusual.

PILEA NUMMULAEIFOLIA (creeping Charlie)

DESCRIPTION: Small circular crenate leaves, pale green; flowers in tiny clusters.

SIZE: To 8 inches

TEMPERATURE: 70°–80°F

HUMIDITY: 20–30 percent

WATERING: Keep evenly moist

LIGHT: Bright

REMARKS: Fine for growing in baskets.

PILEA SERPILLACEA

DESCRIPTION: Succulent branches with orbicular leaves rounded at base; flower clusters stalked.

SIZE: To 10 inches

TEMPERATURE: 70°–80°F

HUMIDITY: 20–30 percent

WATERING: Keep evenly moist

LIGHT: Bright

REMARKS: Good for terrariums or dish gardens.

PILEA SERPILLACEA 'SILVER TREE'

DESCRIPTION: Quilted ovate bronzy-green leaves, broad silver band along center, silver dots on side.

SIZE: To 10 inches

TEMPERATURE: 70°–80°F

HUMIDITY: 20–30 percent

WATERING: Keep evenly moist

LIGHT: Bright

REMARKS: Handsome leaves; use as table or desk plant.

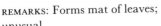

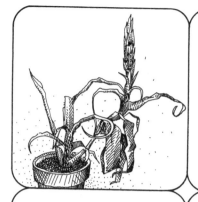

PITCAIRNIA ANDREANA

DESCRIPTION: Leafy stems, green leaves marked with silver dots; orange flowers.

SIZE: To 10 inches

TEMPERATURE: 70°–80°F

HUMIDITY: 30 percent

REMARKS: Give lots of sun; might bloom indoors; another unusual bromeliad.

WATERING: Dry out between waterings

LIGHT: Sun

PLEIONE HOOKERIANA

DESCRIPTION: Pseudobulbs tipped with a few green leaves; flowers rose-colored with a brown-purple splotch.

SIZE: To 8 inches

TEMPERATURE: 65°–75°F

HUMIDITY: 30 percent

REMARKS: An orchid that blooms with little trouble if kept moist and somewhat cool.

WATERING: Keep evenly moist

LIGHT: Bright

PLEIONE PRICEI

DESCRIPTION: Leaves 4 inches high; bears 4-inch solitary flower pale rose with large white-fringed lip.

SIZE: To 4 inches

TEMPERATURE: 65°–75°F

HUMIDITY: 30 percent

REMARKS: Blooms with little trouble if kept moist and somewhat cool.

WATERING: Keep evenly moist

LIGHT: Bright

PLEIOSPILOS LEIPOLDTII

DESCRIPTION: Dark green clumped-shaped leaves covered with dots; yellow flowers.

SIZE: To 2 inches

TEMPERATURE: 72°–80°F

HUMIDITY: 20 percent

REMARKS: Grow with a layer of gravel on top of soil.

WATERING: Dry out between waterings

LIGHT: Sun

PLEIOSPILOS NELII

DESCRIPTION: Split globe with gray thick leaves in pairs with dark dots; yellow flowers.

SIZE: To 2 inches

TEMPERATURE: 72°–80°F

HUMIDITY: 20 percent

REMARKS: Grow with a layer of gravel on top of soil.

WATERING: Dry out between waterings

LIGHT: Sun

157

PLEIOSPILOS PRISMATICUS

DESCRIPTION: Boat-shaped tapering smooth green leaves marked with dots; yellow flowers.

REMARKS: Grow with a layer of gravel on top of soil.

SIZE: To 2 inches

TEMPERATURE: 72°–80°F

HUMIDITY: 20 percent

WATERING: Dry out between waterings

LIGHT: Sun

PLEUROTHALLIS CHRYSANTHA

DESCRIPTION: Leathery spatula leaves, orange flowers.

REMARKS: Has cascading flowers in long stems; nice for basket growing. A fine orchid.

SIZE: To 12 inches

TEMPERATURE: 72°–80°F

HUMIDITY: 40 percent

WATERING: Keep evenly moist

LIGHT: Bright

PLEUROTHALLIS GHIESBREGHTIANA

DESCRIPTION: Solitary green leaves and pendant scapes of yellow flowers.

REMARKS: Cascading orchids on long stems; nice for basket growing.

SIZE: To 14 inches

TEMPERATURE: 72°–80°F

HUMIDITY: 40 percent

WATERING: Keep evenly moist

LIGHT: Bright

PLEUROTHALLIS HOMALANTHA

DESCRIPTION: Solitary leathery leaves, fine yellow flowers.

REMARKS: Cascading orchids on long stems; nice for basket growing.

SIZE: To 14 inches

TEMPERATURE: 72°–80°F

HUMIDITY: 40 percent

WATERING: Keep evenly moist

LIGHT: Bright

PLEUROTHALLIS LONGISSIMA

DESCRIPTION: Slender stems with 5-inch solitary fleshy, oblong, deep green leaves; white flowers tinged yellow.

REMARKS: Cascading orchids on long stems; nice for basket growing.

SIZE: To 14 inches

TEMPERATURE: 72°–80°F

HUMIDITY: 40 percent

WATERING: Keep evenly moist

LIGHT: Bright

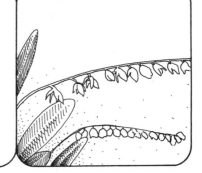

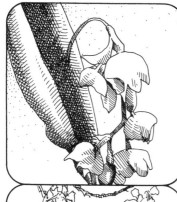

POLYSTACHYA BICARINATA

DESCRIPTION: Orchid with lancelike leaves and waxy pink flowers.

SIZE: To 6 inches

TEMPERATURE: 72°–80°F

HUMIDITY: 30–40 percent

WATERING: Keep evenly moist

LIGHT: Sun

REMARKS: Nice small orchid that requires little care.

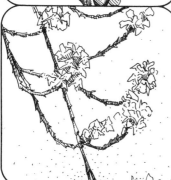

POLYSTACHYA LUTEOLA

DESCRIPTION: Orchid with narrow leaves and small fragrant yellow flowers.

SIZE: To 14 inches

TEMPERATURE: 72°–80°F

HUMIDITY: 30–40 percent

WATERING: Keep evenly moist

LIGHT: Sun

REMARKS: Nice small orchid that requires little care.

POLYSTICHUM TSUS-SIMENSE

DESCRIPTION: Small leathery fern, dark green fronds, sharply toothed.

SIZE: To 10 inches

TEMPERATURE: 72°–85°F

HUMIDITY: 30 percent

WATERING: Keep evenly moist

LIGHT: Shade

REMARKS: Needs an acid soil; add organic matter to soil.

PTERIS CRETICA 'WILSONII' (brake-fern)

DESCRIPTION: Low bushy fern, habit tending to a fan shape.

SIZE: To 10 inches

TEMPERATURE: 72°–80°F

HUMIDITY: 30 percent

WATERING: Keep evenly moist

LIGHT: Bright

REMARKS: Mist foliage frequently; rapid grower under good conditions.

PTERIS ENSIFORMIS 'VICTORIAE'

DESCRIPTION: Erect slender fronds banded white; wavy margin of rich green.

SIZE: To 12 inches

TEMPERATURE: 72°–80°F

HUMIDITY: 30 percent

WATERING: Keep evenly moist

LIGHT: Bright

REMARKS: Mist foliage frequently; rapid grower under good conditions.

PUNICA GRANATUM 'NANA' (pomegranate)

DESCRIPTION: Vivid green narrow leaves, scarlet flowers with salmon calyx, orange-red fruit.

SIZE: To 12 inches

TEMPERATURE: 60°–70°F

HUMIDITY: 50 percent

WATERING: Dry out between waterings

REMARKS: Leaves fall naturally in winter; reduce water somewhat.

LIGHT: Sun

PYROLA ELLIPTICA

DESCRIPTION: Blade-type green leaves, white flowers.

SIZE: To 12 inches

TEMPERATURE: 60°–70°F

HUMIDITY: 20 percent

WATERING: Keep quite moist

REMARKS: A wildflower difficult to cultivate but which sometimes succeeds indoors.

LIGHT: Bright

REBUTIA KUPPERIANA (crown cactus)

DESCRIPTION: Gray-green globe with thin spines; flowers scarlet.

SIZE: To 2 inches

TEMPERATURE: 70°–80°F

HUMIDITY: 30 percent

WATERING: Dry out between waterings

REMARKS: Grow cool (60°F) in winter and reduce watering.

LIGHT: Sun

REBUTIA MINISCULA

DESCRIPTION: Tiny green flattened globe becoming tufted, small whitish spines; flowers scarlet-red.

SIZE: To 2 inches

TEMPERATURE: 70°–80°F

HUMIDITY: 30 percent

WATERING: Dry out between waterings

REMARKS: Grow cool (60°F) in winter and reduce watering.

LIGHT: Sun

REBUTIA SENILIS (fire crown)

DESCRIPTION: Dark green globe covered with white spines; brilliant red blooms.

SIZE: To 2 inches

TEMPERATURE: 70°–80°F

HUMIDITY: 30 percent

WATERING: Dry out between waterings

REMARKS: Grow cool (60°F) in winter and reduce watering.

LIGHT: Sun

RECHSTEINERIA LEUCOTRICHA (Brazilian edelweiss)

DESCRIPTION: Two whorls of large oval leaves covered with silver-white hairs; rose-coral flowers.

REMARKS: After bloom leave tubers in pot and store in dry place at 55°F. In three months repot for next season.

SIZE: To 14 inches

TEMPERATURE: 65°–80°F

HUMIDITY: 50 percent

WATERING: Keep evenly moist

LIGHT: Bright

RECHSTEINERIA MACROPODA

DESCRIPTION: Velvety bright green leaves and small tubular red flowers.

REMARKS: After bloom leave tubers in pot and store in dry place at 55°F. In three months repot for next season.

SIZE: To 9 inches

TEMPERATURE: 65°–80°F

HUMIDITY: 50 percent

WATERING: Keep evenly moist

LIGHT: Bright

RESTREPIA ELEGANS

DESCRIPTION: Single green leaves, small spoon-shaped almost pink flowers.

REMARKS: True miniature orchid that requires little care.

SIZE: To 3 inches

TEMPERATURE: 70°–80°F

HUMIDITY: 30–40 percent

WATERING: Keep evenly moist

LIGHT: Bright

RHIPSALIDOPSIS ROSEA (Easter cactus)

DESCRIPTION: Bushy with small flattened joints, waxy green tinted purple; rosy pink flowers.

REMARKS: Blooms when only a few inches tall.

SIZE: To 6 inches

TEMPERATURE: 70°–80°F

HUMIDITY: 30 percent

WATERING: Keep moist

LIGHT: Sun

RHIPSALIS PARADOXA (chain cactus)

DESCRIPTION: Flat green leaves with sawtooth edges; tiny white flowers.

REMARKS: Pot in equal parts fir bark and soil; grow somewhat dry in winter. Good basket plant.

SIZE: To 20 inches

TEMPERATURE: 60°–75°F

HUMIDITY: 30–40 percent

WATERING: Keep evenly moist

LIGHT: Sun

RHOEO DISCOLOR (Moses-in-a-boat)

DESCRIPTION: Fleshy rosette of stiff, waxy metallic dark green leaves purple beneath; tiny white blooms.

SIZE: To 12 inches

TEMPERATURE: 60°–75°F

HUMIDITY: 30 percent

WATERING: Keep quite moist

REMARKS: Not often seen, but an amenable houseplant.

LIGHT: Bright

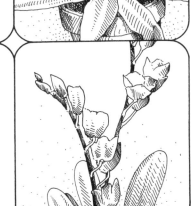

RODRIGUEZIA SECUNDA

DESCRIPTION: Small compressed pseudobulbs, remaining leaves sheathing bulb; rose-red flowers.

SIZE: To 12 inches

TEMPERATURE: 70°–80°F

HUMIDITY: 40 percent

WATERING: Keep evenly moist

REMARKS: Nice small orchid for hanging baskets; give less water in winter.

LIGHT: Sun

RODRIGUEZIA VENUSTA

DESCRIPTION: Narrow leaves and pendant stems of white or rose flowers.

SIZE: To 12 inches

TEMPERATURE: 70°–80°F

HUMIDITY: 40 percent

WATERING: Keep evenly moist

REMARKS: Nice small orchid for hanging baskets; give less water in winter.

LIGHT: Sun

RONNBERGIA COLUMBIANA

DESCRIPTION: Small green-brown leaves, flowers purple-white.

SIZE: To 12 inches

TEMPERATURE: 70°–80°F

HUMIDITY: 30 percent

WATERING: Keep evenly moist

REMARKS: Nice bromeliad for table or desk accent.

LIGHT: Sun

RONNBERGIA MOORENIANA

DESCRIPTION: Small bright green leaves spotted dark green; flowers blue.

SIZE: To 14 inches

TEMPERATURE: 70°–80°F

HUMIDITY: 30 percent

WATERING: Keep evenly moist

REMARKS: Nice bromeliad for table or desk accent.

LIGHT: Sun

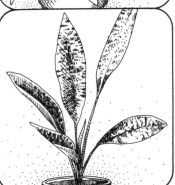

ROSA 'BO PEEP'

DESCRIPTION: Fully double flowers of luscious pink.

REMARKS: Floriferous; good under artificial light.

SIZE: To 6 inches

TEMPERATURE: 65°–75°F

HUMIDITY: 50 percent

WATERING: Keep evenly moist

LIGHT: Sun

ROSA 'CINDERELLA'

DESCRIPTION: Double white flowers tinged pink.

REMARKS: Good plant but likes cool conditions.

SIZE: To 6 inches

TEMPERATURE: 65°–75°F

HUMIDITY: 50 percent

WATERING: Keep evenly moist

LIGHT: Sun

ROSA 'DARLING FLAME'

DESCRIPTION: New variety with red-orange flowers.

REMARKS: Stays quite small; compact growth.

SIZE: To 8 inches

TEMPERATURE: 65°–75°F

HUMIDITY: 50 percent

WATERING: Keep evenly moist

LIGHT: Sun

ROSA 'FIRE PRINCESS'

DESCRIPTION: Fiery orange-red flowers.

REMARKS: Blooms when very small; excellent for beginners.

SIZE: To 3 inches

TEMPERATURE: 65°–75°F

HUMIDITY: 50 percent

WATERING: Keep evenly moist

LIGHT: Sun

ROSA 'LITTLE CHIEF'

DESCRIPTION: Recent introduction; vivid red flowers.

REMARKS: Excellent variety and makes a fine pot plant for table or desk.

SIZE: To 2 inches

TEMPERATURE: 65°–75°F

HUMIDITY: 50 percent

WATERING: Keep evenly moist

LIGHT: Sun

ROSA 'MARY ADAIR'

DESCRIPTION: Has apricot flowers on a dense compact bush.

SIZE: To 14 inches

TEMPERATURE: 65°–75°F

HUMIDITY: 50 percent

WATERING: Keep evenly moist

LIGHT: Sun

REMARKS: Fine plant that does well under artificial light.

ROSA 'MARY MARSHALL'

DESCRIPTION: Small orange flowers, fragrant.

SIZE: To 14 inches

TEMPERATURE: 65°–75°F

HUMIDITY: 50 percent

WATERING: Keep evenly moist

LIGHT: Sun

REMARKS: Very tiny and very fragrant; somewhat difficult to grow.

ROSA 'NANCY HALL'

DESCRIPTION: Compact plant; flowers an unusual shade of peach.

SIZE: To 14 inches

TEMPERATURE: 65°–75°F

HUMIDITY: 30 percent

WATERING: Keep evenly moist

LIGHT: Sun

REMARKS: Good indoor grower.

ROSA 'PEACHY WHITE'

DESCRIPTION: Produces an exceptional abundance of pink flowers.

SIZE: To 8 inches

TEMPERATURE: 65°–75°F

HUMIDITY: 30 percent

WATERING: Keep evenly moist

LIGHT: Sun

REMARKS: An award winner; floriferous.

ROSA 'RED IMP'

DESCRIPTION: Smallest red miniature rose.

SIZE: To 4 inches

TEMPERATURE: 65°–75°F

HUMIDITY: 30 percent

WATERING: Keep evenly moist

LIGHT: Sun

REMARKS Very tiny and very popular.

ROSA 'SMALL WORLD'

DESCRIPTION: Has small blooms of clear, intense crimson.

SIZE: To 4 inches

TEMPERATURE: 65°–75°F

HUMIDITY: 50 percent

WATERING: Keep evenly moist

REMARKS: One of the best of the tiny roses; does well indoors.

LIGHT: Sun

ROSA 'STARINA'

DESCRIPTION: Quilted petals of deep, orange-red.

SIZE: To 8 inches

TEMPERATURE: 65°–75°F

HUMIDITY: 50 percent

WATERING: Keep evenly moist

REMARKS: One of the best of the tiny roses; does well indoors.

LIGHT: Sun

SAINTPAULIA 'DOUBLE DUMPLING'

DESCRIPTION: Ruffled red-violet to wine notched leaf. Fine blue flowers.

SIZE: To 5 inches

TEMPERATURE: 70°–80°F

HUMIDITY: 30 percent

WATERING: Keep evenly moist

REMARKS: Very attractive foliage.

LIGHT: Bright

SAINTPAULIA 'HONEYETTE'

DESCRIPTION: Girl-type leaves form a perfect circle. Double, reddish-orchid bicolored flowers.

SIZE: To 4 inches

TEMPERATURE: 70°–80°F

HUMIDITY: 30 percent

WATERING: Keep evenly moist

REMARKS: Blooms very small.

LIGHT: Bright

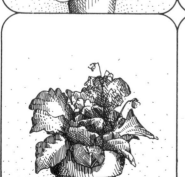

SAINTPAULIA 'LAVENDER ELFIN GIRL'

DESCRIPTION: Leaves are fluted and ruffled; lavender single flowers.

SIZE: To 4 inches

TEMPERATURE: 70°–80°F

HUMIDITY: 30 percent

WATERING: Keep evenly moist

REMARKS: A longtime favorite.

LIGHT: Bright

SAINTPAULIA 'LULA BELL'

DESCRIPTION: Beautiful foliage and handsome blue flowers.

REMARKS: Another good miniature African violet.

SIZE: To 5 inches

TEMPERATURE: 70°–80°F

HUMIDITY: 30 percent

WATERING: Keep evenly moist

LIGHT: Bright

SAINTPAULIA 'MINIATURE SAILOR GIRL'

DESCRIPTION: Girl-type leaves, heavily quilted and spooned; blue flowers.

REMARKS: Always good for indoor color.

SIZE: To 4 inches

TEMPERATURE: 70°–80°F

HUMIDITY: 30 percent

WATERING: Keep evenly moist

LIGHT: Bright

SAINTPAULIA 'MINNEAPOLIS'

DESCRIPTION: Bright double pink flowers, plain green leaves.

REMARKS: Another good African violet.

SIZE: To 4 inches

TEMPERATURE: 70°–80°F.

HUMIDITY: 30 percent

WATERING: Keep evenly moist

LIGHT: Bright

SAINTPAULIA 'ORCHID ELFIN GIRL'

DESCRIPTION: Spooned, scalloped foliage, orchid flowers sometimes tinted blue.

REMARKS: Beautiful winter color.

SIZE: To 4 inches

TEMPERATURE: 70°–80°F

HUMIDITY: 30 percent

WATERING: Keep evenly moist

LIGHT: Bright

SAINTPAULIA 'PINK ROCK'

DESCRIPTION: Heavily quilted leaves, pink flowers.

REMARKS: Good pink color.

SIZE: To 6 inches

TEMPERATURE: 70°–80°F

HUMIDITY: 30 percent

WATERING: Keep evenly moist

LIGHT: Bright

SAINTPAULIA 'SWEET SIXTEEN'

DESCRIPTION: Large double white flowers.

SIZE: To 4 inches

TEMPERATURE: 70°–80°F

HUMIDITY: 30 percent

WATERING: Keep evenly moist

REMARKS: Has handsome foliage.

LIGHT: Bright

SAINTPAULIA 'TINKLE'

DESCRIPTION: Ruffled leaves; double lavender flowers.

SIZE: To 4 inches

TEMPERATURE: 70°–80°F

HUMIDITY: 30 percent

WATERING: Keep evenly moist

REMARKS: A true miniature and a good one.

LIGHT: Bright

SAINTPAULIA 'TINY BELLS'

DESCRIPTION: Quilted and fluted dark green leaves; dark blue flowers.

SIZE: To 4 inches

TEMPERATURE: 70°–80°F

HUMIDITY: 30 percent

WATERING: Keep evenly moist

REMARKS: Fine blue flowers.

LIGHT: Bright

SAINTPAULIA 'WENDY'

DESCRIPTION: Large single blue flowers.

SIZE: To 5 inches

TEMPERATURE: 70°–80°F

HUMIDITY: 30 percent

WATERING: Keep evenly moist

REMARKS: Another good African violet.

LIGHT: Bright

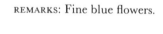

SAINTPAULIA 'WHITE DOLL'

DESCRIPTION: Girl-type leaves; white single flowers.

SIZE: To 4 inches

TEMPERATURE: 70°–80°F

HUMIDITY: 30 percent

WATERING: Keep evenly moist

REMARKS: Blooms when very small.

LIGHT: Bright

SANSEVIERIA 'GOLDEN HAHNII'

DESCRIPTION: Firm, broad leathery leaves in low rosette, broad cream to yellow bands alongside margin.

SIZE: To 8 inches

TEMPERATURE: 72°–80°F

HUMIDITY: 30 percent

WATERING: Keep evenly moist

LIGHT: Bright

REMARKS: Will survive shade if necessary; slow growing.

SASA PYGMYAEA

DESCRIPTION: Dense clumps; small leathery, deep green leaves.

SIZE: To 10 inches

TEMPERATURE: 72°–80°F

HUMIDITY: 30–40 percent

WATERING: Keep quite moist

LIGHT: Bright

REMARKS: Drops leaves but still a good indoor plant.

SAXIFRAGA COTYLEDON

DESCRIPTION: Gray-green leaves tinged with red; handsome rosette-type plant.

SIZE: To 5 inches

TEMPERATURE: 65°–75°F

HUMIDITY: 30 percent

WATERING: Keep evenly moist

LIGHT: Bright

REMARKS: Dies down in winter; reduce watering. Start again in new soil in early spring.

SAXIFRAGA GRANULATA

DESCRIPTION: Lobed leaves; white flowers.

SIZE: To 20 inches

TEMPERATURE: 60°–70°F

HUMIDITY: 30 percent

WATERING: Keep evenly moist

LIGHT: Bright

REMARKS: Makes unusual pot plant, but pretty.

SAXIFRAGA SARMENTOSA (strawberry geranium)

DESCRIPTION: Fleshy, rounded hairy leaves, deep olive green with purple beneath.

SIZE: To 6 inches

TEMPERATURE: 65°–75°F

HUMIDITY: 30 percent

WATERING: Keep evenly moist

LIGHT: Bright

REMARKS: Very popular and rightly so; an excellent houseplant.

SAXIFRAGA SARMENTOSA 'TRICOLOR'

DESCRIPTION: Small dark green leaves marked with white and tinted with pink.

REMARKS: A fine hybrid; slightly more difficult to grow than others in the group.

SIZE: To 8 inches

TEMPERATURE: 75°–85°F

HUMIDITY: 30 percent

WATERING: Keep evenly moist

LIGHT: Bright

SCHIZOCENTRON ELEGANS (Spanish shawl)

DESCRIPTION: Oval dark green hairy leaves, purple flowers.

REMARKS: Needs some extra attention but worth it; blooms on and off throughout the year.

SIZE: To 10 inches (trailer)

TEMPERATURE: 65°–80°F

HUMIDITY: 30 percent

WATERING: Keep evenly moist

LIGHT: Bright

SCILLA VIOLACEA

DESCRIPTION: Somewhat fleshy leaves; flowers green with white and purple.

REMARKS: Outdoor bulb that can be grown in pots indoors.

SIZE: To 6 inches

TEMPERATURE: 60°–70°F

HUMIDITY: 30 percent

WATERING: Keep quite moist

LIGHT: Bright

SEDUM ADOLPHI

DESCRIPTION: Plump fleshy leaves, waxy yellowish-green with reddish margins.

REMARKS: Easy to grow plant.

SIZE: To 4 inches

TEMPERATURE: 70°–80°F

HUMIDITY: 20 percent

WATERING: Dry out between waterings

LIGHT: Sun

SEDUM CUSPIDATUM

DESCRIPTION: Branching plant with flat oval green leaves.

REMARKS: Good basket plant.

SIZE: To 12 inches

TEMPERATURE: 70°–80°F

HUMIDITY: 20 percent

WATERING: Dry out between waterings

LIGHT: Sun

SEDUM DASYPHYLLUM

DESCRIPTION: Fleshy oval tiny blue-green leaves, white flowers.

REMARKS: Unusual appearance; makes a fine trailing plant.

SIZE: To 4 inches

TEMPERATURE: 70°–80°F

HUMIDITY: 20 percent

WATERING: Dry out between waterings

LIGHT: Sun

SEDUM LINEARE

DESCRIPTION: Turf-forming succulent with small soft gray-green fleshy leaves with white margins.

REMARKS: a handsome rosette plant; makes good table accent.

SIZE: To 4 inches

TEMPERATURE: 70°–80°F

HUMIDITY: 20 percent

WATERING: Dry out between waterings

LIGHT: Sun

SEDUM RUBROTINCTUM (Christmas cheer)

DESCRIPTION: Small branching succulent; glossy green club-shaped leaves, yellow flowers.

REMARKS: Nothing spectacular but grows easily.

SIZE: To 8 inches (across)

TEMPERATURE: 70°–80°F

HUMIDITY: 20 percent

WATERING: Dry out between waterings

LIGHT: Sun

SEDUM SPURIUM

DESCRIPTION: Small succulent with thin flexible reddish stems, red to white flowers.

REMARKS: Handsome; makes beautiful indoor subject.

SIZE: To 8 inches

TEMPERATURE: 70°–80°F

HUMIDITY: 20 percent

WATERING: Dry out between waterings

LIGHT: Sun

SELAGINELLA KRAUSSIANA BROWNI

DESCRIPTION: Mosslike cushions of densely clustering short branches of vivid emerald green.

REMARKS: Small and dainty; a cascade of green.

SIZE: To 6 inches

TEMPERATURE: 65°–75°F

HUMIDITY: 30 percent

WATERING: Keep evenly moist

LIGHT: Bright

170

SELAGINELLA UNCINATA

DESCRIPTION: Low creeper with straw-colored rambling stems.

REMARKS: Creeping habit; best for basket growing.

SIZE: To 10 inches

TEMPERATURE: 70°–80°F

HUMIDITY: 30 percent

WATERING: Keep evenly moist

LIGHT: Bright

SEMPERVIVUM ARACHNOIDEUM (cobweb houseleek)

DESCRIPTION: Tiny rosettes forming mounds covered with white hairs; reddish flowers.

REMARKS: Beautiful in dish gardens.

SIZE: To 2 inches

TEMPERATURE: 70°–80°F

HUMIDITY: 20 percent

WATERING: Keep somewhat dry

LIGHT: Bright

SEMPERVIVUM MONTANUM

DESCRIPTION: Plain green oval leaves, yellowish-white flowers.

REMARKS: Beautiful color; good for dish gardens.

SIZE: To 6 inches

TEMPERATURE: 60°–70°F

HUMIDITY: 20 percent

WATERING: Keep evenly moist

LIGHT: Sun

SEMPERVIVUM TECTORUM CALCAREUM

DESCRIPTION: Small leathery rosettes forming clusters; light gray-green leaves.

REMARKS: Beautiful foliage plant.

SIZE: To 12 inches (across)

TEMPERATURE: 60°–70°F

HUMIDITY: 20 percent

WATERING: Keep evenly moist

LIGHT: Sun

SIDERASIS FUSCATA

DESCRIPTION: Broad olive green leaves with a silver band and covered with brown hairs.

REMARKS: Do not get water on leaves.

SIZE: To 12 inches

TEMPERATURE: 75°–85°F

HUMIDITY: 40 percent

WATERING: Keep evenly moist

LIGHT: Shade

SINNINGIA PUSILLA

DESCRIPTION: Little oval puckered leaves, olive green with brown veins; orchid color flower.

REMARKS: Exquisite miniature; don't miss it.

SIZE: To 2 inches

TEMPERATURE: 65°–75°F

HUMIDITY: 20 percent

WATERING: Keep evenly moist

LIGHT: Bright

SINNINGIA PUSILLA 'DOLL BABY'

DESCRIPTION: Oval puckered leaves olive green with brown veins; white flowers.

REMARKS: Another exceptional miniature plant.

SIZE: To 2 inches

TEMPERATURE: 65° -75°F

HUMIDITY: 20 percent

WATERING: Keep evenly moist

LIGHT: Bright

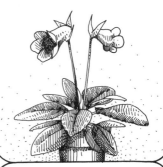

SINNINGIA PUSILLA 'PRISCILLA'

DESCRIPTION: Oval puckered leaves olive green with brown veins; pink flowers.

REMARKS: One of the best miniature plants.

SIZE: To 2 inches

TEMPERATURE: 65°–75°F

HUMIDITY: 20 percent

WATERING: Keep evenly moist

LIGHT: Bright

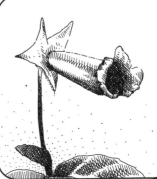

SINNINGIA PUSILLA 'WOOD NYMPH'

DESCRIPTION: Oval puckered leaves olive green with brown veins; lavender flowers.

REMARKS: Another good miniature plant.

SIZE: To 2 inches

TEMPERATURE: 65°–75°F

HUMIDITY: 20 percent

WATERING: Keep evenly moist

LIGHT: Bright

SISYRINCHIUM IRIDIFOLIUM (blue-eyed grass)

DESCRIPTION: Grassy leaves with yellowish-white flowers.

REMARKS: An outdoor plant that can be grown indoors.

SIZE: To 14 inches

TEMPERATURE: 60°–70°F

HUMIDITY: 20 percent

WATERING: Keep evenly moist

LIGHT: Bright

SMITHIANTHA CINNABARINA

DESCRIPTION: Red plush heart-shaped leaves and scarlet bell-shaped flowers.

SIZE: To 10 inches

TEMPERATURE: 75°–85°F

HUMIDITY: 40 percent

WATERING: Keep evenly moist

REMARKS: Don't get water on foliage.

LIGHT: Shade

SMITHIANTHA ZEBRINA

DESCRIPTION: Handsome heart-shaped leaves, orange-red flowers.

SIZE: To 10 inches

TEMPERATURE: 75°–85°F

HUMIDITY: 40 percent

WATERING: Keep evenly moist

REMARKS: Don't get water on leaves.

LIGHT: Shade

SONERILA MARGARITACEA

DESCRIPTION: Deep coppery-green leaves, red-purple beneath, and rosy-lavender flowers.

SIZE: To 8 inches

TEMPERATURE: 75°–85°F

HUMIDITY: 40 percent

WATERING: Keep evenly moist

REMARKS: Handsome foliage plant.

LIGHT: Bright

SONERILA MARGARITACEA ARGENTEA

DESCRIPTION: Pointed leaves overlaid with silver.

SIZE: To 8 inches

TEMPERATURE: 75°–85°F

HUMIDITY: 40 percent

WATERING: Keep evenly moist

REMARKS: Lovely foliage plant.

LIGHT: Bright

SONERILA MARGARITACEA HENDERSONII

DESCRIPTION: Dainty coppery-red foliage covered with silver spots, purple underneath.

SIZE: To 8 inches

TEMPERATURE: 75°–85°F

HUMIDITY: 40 percent

WATERING: Keep evenly moist

REMARKS: Grown for its handsome foliage.

LIGHT: Bright

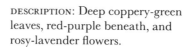

SOPHRONITIS CERNUA

DESCRIPTION: Pseudobulbs that bear a solitary leathery leaf; orange-red flower.

REMARKS: Very large flowers; a stunning plant.

SIZE: To 3 inches

TEMPERATURE: 60°–70°F

HUMIDITY: 30 percent

WATERING: Keep evenly moist

LIGHT: Shade

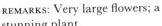

SOPHRONITIS GRANDIFLORA

DESCRIPTION: Small pseudobulbs that bear a solitary leathery leaf; flower bright red.

REMARKS: Exquisite large flowers. Excellent plant.

SIZE: To 3 inches

TEMPERATURE: 60°–70°F

HUMIDITY: 30 percent

WATERING: Keep evenly moist

LIGHT: Shade

SPARAXIS GRANDIFLORA

DESCRIPTION: Fanlike foliage and large purple or yellow flowers.

REMARKS: Grow in pots; excellent for cut flowers.

SIZE: To 14 inches

TEMPERATURE: 60°–70°F

HUMIDITY: 30 percent

WATERING: Keep evenly moist

LIGHT: Sun

SPARAXIS TRICOLOR

DESCRIPTION: Sword-shaped leaves, orange flowers tipped with brown-purple.

REMARKS: Really very pretty cut flowers; grow in pots.

SIZE: To 14 inches

TEMPERATURE: 60°–70°F

HUMIDITY: 30 percent

WATERING: Keep evenly moist

LIGHT: Sun

STENANDRIUM LINDENII

DESCRIPTION: Coppery-green leaves, yellow-green vein area, purplish beneath.

REMARKS: Grown for its exquisite foliage.

SIZE: To 12 inches

TEMPERATURE: 75°–85°F

HUMIDITY: 30 percent

WATERING: Keep evenly moist

LIGHT: Shade

STREPTOCARPUS REXII (cape primrose)

DESCRIPTION: Small stemless plant with long narrow leaves in rosettes, pale lavender flowers.

SIZE: To 12 inches

TEMPERATURE: 70°–80°F

HUMIDITY: 30 percent

WATERING: Keep evenly moist

REMARKS: Large handsome flowers make this one worthwhile.

LIGHT: Bright

STREPTOCARPUS SAXORUM

DESCRIPTION: Fleshy leaves in whorls; flowers with white tube, lilac lobes.

SIZE: To 12 inches

TEMPERATURE: 70°–80°F

HUMIDITY: 30 percent

WATERING: Keep evenly moist

REMARKS: Good flowering plant for indoors.

LIGHT: Bright

SYNGONIUM PODOPHYLLUM (arrowhead plant)

DESCRIPTION: Arrow-shaped thin green leaves, scandent habit.

SIZE: To 14 inches

TEMPERATURE: 70°–80°F

HUMIDITY: 20 percent

WATERING: Dry out between waterings

REMARKS: Grows like a weed.

LIGHT: Bright

TILLANDSIA IONANTHE

DESCRIPTION: Rosette with tufted leaves, green with silvery bristles; violet flowers.

SIZE: To 3 inches

TEMPERATURE: 70°–80°F

HUMIDITY: 20 percent

WATERING: Keep evenly moist

REMARKS: An excellent bromeliad best grown on slab of bark.

LIGHT: Sun

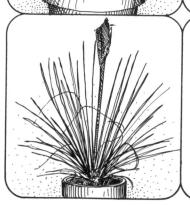

TILLANDSIA JUNCEA

DESCRIPTION: Grayish-green leaves, rosette habit.

SIZE: To 12 inches

TEMPERATURE: 70°–80°F

HUMIDITY: 20 percent

REMARKS: Larger bromeliad than T. ionanthe and not as colorful, but still good.

WATERING: Keep evenly moist

LIGHT: Sun

TRADESCANTIA LAEKENSIS

DESCRIPTION: Pale green leaves with white stripes and bands of purple; white flowers.

REMARKS: Good trailing plant for baskets.

SIZE: To 14 inches

TEMPERATURE: 70°–80°F

HUMIDITY: 20 percent

WATERING: Keep evenly moist

LIGHT: Bright

TRADESCANTIA MULTIFLORA (Tahitian bridal veil)

DESCRIPTION: Stringlike stems and narrow shiny green leaves; trailing habit.

REMARKS: Also known as Gibasis multiflora.

SIZE: To 14 inches

TEMPERATURE: 70°–80°F

HUMIDITY: 20 percent

WATERING: Keep evenly moist

LIGHT: Bright

TRICHOPILIA ELEGANS

DESCRIPTION: Papery dark green leaves and large white flowers.

REMARKS: Elegant orchid with flowers that last several weeks.

SIZE: To 12 inches

TEMPERATURE: 70°–80°F

HUMIDITY: 30 percent

WATERING: Keep evenly moist

LIGHT: Bright

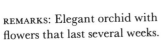

TRICHOPILIA MARGINATA

DESCRIPTION: Narrow leaves and trumpet-shaped flowers; brownish-red petals, marked creamy white.

REMARKS: Most beautiful of the trichopilias orchids.

SIZE: To 12 inches

TEMPERATURE: 70°–80°F

HUMIDITY: 30 percent

WATERING: Keep evenly moist

LIGHT: Bright

TRICHOPILIA TORTILIS

DESCRIPTION: Large papery dark green leaves and large creamy white flowers.

REMARKS: Very large orchid flowers for size of plant.

SIZE: To 12 inches

TEMPERATURE: 70°–80°F

HUMIDITY: 30 percent

WATERING: Keep evenly moist

LIGHT: Sun

TULIPA BIFLORA

DESCRIPTION: Flowers almost white but lightly marked with green and crimson.

REMARKS: Grow in pots for window color.

SIZE: To 12 inches

TEMPERATURE: 60°–70°F

HUMIDITY: 20 percent

WATERING: Keep evenly moist

LIGHT: Sun

TULIPA CHRYSANTHA

DESCRIPTION: Large flowers, creamy white on inside with yellow tinge, red markings.

REMARKS: Good outdoor bulbous plant for indoor color.

SIZE: To 10 inches

TEMPERATURE: 60°–70°F

HUMIDITY: 20 percent

WATERING: Keep evenly moist

LIGHT: Sun

TULIPA KAUFMANNIANA

DESCRIPTION: Star-shaped solitary flowers, yellowish-white, red-margined.

REMARKS: Most popular of the small tulips.

SIZE: To 6 inches

TEMPERATURE: 60°–70°F

HUMIDITY: 20 percent

WATERING: Keep evenly moist

LIGHT: Sun

TULIPA TARDA

DESCRIPTION: Rosette of grassy green leaves, star-shaped flowers marked green and red.

REMARKS: Good small outdoor tulip for growing in pots.

SIZE: To 4 inches

TEMPERATURE: 60°–70°F

HUMIDITY: 20 percent

WATERING: Keep evenly moist

LIGHT: Sun

TULIPA TURKESTANICA

DESCRIPTION: Narrow leaves, star-shaped ivory-white flowers with orange base.

REMARKS: Another fine tulip for indoor growing.

SIZE: To 6 inches

TEMPERATURE: 60°–70°F

HUMIDITY: 20 percent

WATERING: Keep evenly moist

LIGHT: Sun

VALLOTA SPECIOSA (Scarborough lily)

DESCRIPTION: Straplike leaves and scarlet funnel-shaped flowers.

SIZE: To 14 inches

TEMPERATURE: 70°–80°F

HUMIDITY: 20 percent

WATERING: Keep evenly moist

LIGHT: Bright

REMARKS: Reduce watering somewhat after bloom.

VANDA CRISTATA

DESCRIPTION: Leathery straplike leaves and handsome yellowish-green flowers tinged red.

SIZE: To 12 inches

TEMPERATURE: 75°–85°F

HUMIDITY: 30 percent

WATERING: Dry out between waterings

LIGHT: Sun

REMARKS: One of the few true small vanda orchids.

VIOLA CANADENSIS

DESCRIPTION: Toothed leaves, white and yellow flowers.

SIZE: To 12 inches

TEMPERATURE: 60°–70°F

HUMIDITY: 30 percent

WATERING: Keep evenly moist

LIGHT: Bright

REMARKS: An outdoor plant; worth a try indoors.

VIOLA PEDATA

DESCRIPTION: Divided leaves, toothed; dark violet flowers.

SIZE: To 6 inches

TEMPERATURE: 60°–70°F

HUMIDITY: 30 percent

WATERING: Keep evenly moist

LIGHT: Bright

REMARKS: A wildflower; worth a try indoors.

VRIESEA BARILLETTII

DESCRIPTION: Small rosette of pale green leaves; purple bracts.

SIZE: To 10 inches

TEMPERATURE: 70°–80°F

HUMIDITY: 20 percent

WATERING: Keep evenly moist

LIGHT: Sun

REMARKS: Good small bromeliad; easy to grow.

VRIESEA CARINATA

DESCRIPTION: Pale green foliage, yellow and red flower bracts.

SIZE: To 10 inches

TEMPERATURE: 70°–80°F

HUMIDITY: 20 percent

REMARKS: A favorite bromeliad; holds color a long time.

WATERING: Keep evenly moist

LIGHT: Sun

VRIESEA 'MARIAE' (painted feather)

DESCRIPTION: Light green foliage, featherlike flower spike, salmon-rose.

SIZE: To 12 inches

TEMPERATURE: 75°–85°F

HUMIDITY: 20 percent

REMARKS: Flower bracts hold color for several weeks.

WATERING: Keep evenly moist

LIGHT: Sun

VRIESEA SPLENDENS (flaming sword)

DESCRIPTION: Bluish-green leaves with purple bands, orange flowers bracts.

SIZE: To 10 inches

TEMPERATURE: 75°–85°F

HUMIDITY: 20 percent

REMARKS: Another good small bromeliad.

WATERING: Keep evenly moist

LIGHT: Sun

XANTHOSOMA LINDENII

DESCRIPTION: Green arrow-shaped leaves beautifully marked with white.

SIZE: To 12 inches

TEMPERATURE: 75°–85°F

HUMIDITY: 40 percent

REMARKS: A jungle denizen; likes warmth and moisture.

WATERING: Keep evenly moist

LIGHT: Shade

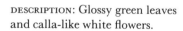

ZANTEDESCHIA AETHIOPECA

DESCRIPTION: Glossy green leaves and calla-like white flowers.

SIZE: To 10 inches

TEMPERATURE: 65°–75°F

HUMIDITY: 20 percent

REMARKS: Outdoor plant that does well indoors.

WATERING: Keep evenly moist

LIGHT: Bright

ZANTEDESCHIA ELLIOTTIANA (yellow calla-lily)

DESCRIPTION: Bright green leaves with white spots, yellow flowers.

SIZE: To 10 inches

TEMPERATURE: 65°–75°F

HUMIDITY: 20 percent

WATERING: Keep evenly moist

LIGHT: Bright

REMARKS: Handsome; good for cut flowers.

ZANTEDESCHIA REHMANNII

DESCRIPTION: Bright green leaves with white spots, pink flowers.

SIZE: To 10 inches

TEMPERATURE: 65°–75°F

HUMIDITY: 20 percent

WATERING: Keep evenly moist

LIGHT: Bright

REMARKS: The most popular of the miniature calla-lilies.

ZEPHYRANTHES CANDIDA

DESCRIPTION: Grassy leaves and white flowers.

SIZE: To 8 inches

TEMPERATURE: 70°–80°F

HUMIDITY: 20 percent

WATERING: Keep evenly moist

LIGHT: Sun

REMARKS: Good bulbous plant; does well indoors.

ZEPHYRANTHES GRANDIFLORA

DESCRIPTION: Green leaves, large pink funnel-shaped flowers.

SIZE: To 8 inches

TEMPERATURE: 70°–80°F

HUMIDITY: 20 percent

WATERING: Keep evenly moist

LIGHT: Sun

REMARKS: Good bulbous plant; does well indoors.

ZYGOPETALUM CRINITUM

DESCRIPTION: Apple green leaves, fragrant greenish-brown flowers, white lip streaked violet-blue.

SIZE: To 12 inches

TEMPERATURE: 65°–75°F

HUMIDITY: 30 percent

WATERING: Dry out between waterings

LIGHT: Shade

REMARKS: Fine small orchids with exotic flowers.

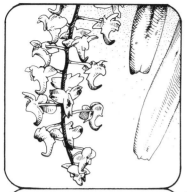

Appendices

The mail-order suppliers below carry all types of small and miniature plants. Almost every one will furnish a catalogue, but many do make a nominal charge for it. The fee is usually refundable, though, on the first purchase of plants.

Alberts & Merkel Bros. Inc.
2210 S. Federal Highway
Boynton Beach, FL 33435

Arthur Eames Allgrove
Box 459
Wilmington, MA 01887

Barrington Greenhouses
860 Clemente Rd.
Barrington, NJ 08016

Buell's Greenhouses
Eastford, CT 06242

Cactus by Mueller
10411 Rosedale Highway
Bakersfield, CA 93307

Cooks Geranium Nursery
712 N. Grand
Lyons, KS 67554

Fischer's Greenhouses
Dept. HC
Linwood, NJ 08221

Henrietta's Cactus Nursery
1345 N. Brawley
Fresno, CA 93705

Ilgenfritz, Margaret, Orchids
Monroe, MI 48161

Logee's Greenhouses
55 North St.
Danielson, CT 06239

Lyon, Lyndon
14 Multcher St.
Dolgeville, NY 13329

Merry Gardens
Camden, ME 04843

Oak Hill Gardens
Binnie Road
Dundee, IL 60118

Tinari Greenhouses
2325 Valley Rd.
Huntington Valley, PA
19006

BOTANICAL NAME/COMMON NAME CROSS REFERENCE

Acorus gramineus	Flag plant
Adiantum cuneatum gracillimum	Maidenhair fern
Adromischus cooperi	Plover eggs
A. masculatus	Calico hearts
Aglaonema commutatum	Chinese evergreen
Allophytum mexicanum	Mexican foxglove
Aloe aristata	Lace aloe
A. nobilis	Gold-eyed aloe
A. variegata	Partridge breast aloe
Arisaema triphyllum	Jack-in-the-pulpit
Asplenium platyneuron	Spleenwort
A. trichomanes	Maidenhair spleenwort
Bambusa nana	Miniature bamboo
Begonia boweri	Eyelash begonia
B. dregei	Maple-leaf begonia
B. foliosa	Fern begonia
B. hydrocotylifolia	Pennywort begonia
Billbergia nutans	Queen's tears
Brassavola nodosa	Lady-of-the-night
Campanula elatines	Star-of-Bethlehem
Camptosorus rhizophyllus	Walking fern
Carsissa grandiflora 'Nana'	Natal plum
Cephalocereus palmeri	Wooly torch
C. polylophus	Aztec column

C. senilis	old man cactus
Ceropegia woodii	string-of-hearts
Chamacereus silvestrii	peanut cactus
Chrysanthemum frutescens	florist chrysanthemum
Citrus taitensis	otahetie prange
Cleistocactus baumannii	scarlet bugler
C. strausii	silver torch
Colchicum autumnale	autumn crocus
C. bulbocodium	meadow saffron
Convallaria majalis	lily-of-the-valley
Coptis trifolia	goldenthread
Crassula arborescens	silver dollar plant
C. deltoidea	silver beads
Cyanotis somaliense	pussy ears
Cymbalaria muralis	kenilworth ivy
Cypripedium parviflorum	ladyslipper orchid
C. pubescens	ladyslipper orchid
Cyrtomium falcatum	holly fern
Davallia bullata mariesii	rabbit's foot fern
Dionese muscipula	Venus flytrap
Drosera rotundifolia	sundew
Echeveria derenbergii	painted lady
Echeveria elegans	Mexican snowball
Echinocactus grusoni	golden barrel
Echinocereus reichenbehii	Lace cactus
Echinopsis multiplex	Barrel cactus
Epigaea repens	Trailing arbutus
Eucharis grandiflora	Amazon lily
Eucomis punctata	Pineapple plant
Euphorbia obesa	Basketball plant
Exacum affine	German violet
Faucaria tigrina	Tiger's jaws
Fenestraria aurantiaca	Window plant
Fenestraria rhopalophylla	Window plant
Ficus pumila	Creeping fig
Fortunella hindsii	Kumquat
Fragaria indica	Mock strawberry
Galanthus nivalis	Snowdrops
Gasteria maculata	Ox-tongue plant
Goodyera pubescens	Rattlesnake plant
Gymnocalycium mihanovichi	Chin cactus
Hedera helix	Ivy
Humata tyermannii	Bear's foot fern
Hypocyrta nummularia	Goldfish plant

Hypoestes sanguinolata	Polka dot plant
Kaempferia roscoeana	Peacock plant
Kalanchoe tomentosa	Panda plant
Lithops bella	Living stones
Malpighia coccigera	Miniature Holly
Mammillaria bocasana	Pincushion cactus
Mammillaria hahniana	Old lady cactus
Manettia bicolor	Mexican firecracker
Maranata massangeana	Prayer plant
Masdevallia coccinea	Kite orchid
Muehleneckia complexa	Wireplant
Muscari armeniacum	Grape hyacinth
Nepeta cataritica	Catnip
Notocactus submannulosus	Lemon ball
Opuntia basilaris	Beaver-pad cactus
Opuntia erinacea	Grizzly bear
Opuntia microdasys	Bunny ears
Oxalis cernua	Bermuda buttercup
Oxalis hedysaroides	Firefern
Parodia aureispina	Tom Thumb cactus
Pellaea rotundifolia	Button fern
Peperomia sandersii	Watermelon peperomia
Pilea cadierei 'minima'	Aluminum plant
Pilea microphylla	Artillery plant
Pilea nummulaeifolia	Creeping Charlie
Pteris cretica 'Wilsonii'	Brake-fern
Punica granatum 'Nana'	Pomegranate
Rebutia kupperiana	Crown cactus
Retutia senilis	Fire crown
Rechsteineria leucotricha	Brazilian edelweiss
Rhipsalis paradoxa	Chain cactus
Rhoeo discolor	Moses-in-a-boat
Rosa	Rose
Saintpaulia	African violet
Saxifraga sarmentosa	Strawberry geranium
Schizocentron elegans	Spanish shawl
Sedum rubrotinctum	Christmas cheer
Sempervivum arachnoideum	Cobweb houseleek
Sisyrinchium iridifolium	Blue-eyed grass
Smithiantha connabrina	Temple bells
Syngonium podophyllum	Arrowhead plant
Tradescantia multiflora	Tahitian bridal veil
Tulipa	Tulip
Vallota speciosa	Scarborough lily

Vreisea 'Mariae'   Painted feather

Vriesea splendens   Flaming sword

Zantedeschia elliottiana   Yellow calla-lily

African violet	*Saintpaulia*
Aluminum plant	*Pilea cadierei 'Mimima'*
Amazon lily	*Eucharis grandiflora*
Arrowhead plant	*Syngonium podophyllum*
Artillary plant	*Pilea microphylla*
Autumn crocus	*Colchicum autumnale*
Aztec column	*Cephalocereua polylophus*
Barrel cactus	*Echinopsis multiplex*
Basketball plant	*Euphorbia obesa*
Bear's foot fern	*Humata tyermannii*
Beaver pad cactus	*Opuntia basilaris*
Bermuda buttercup	*Oxalis cernua*
Blue-eyed grass	*Sisylinchium iridifolium*
Brake-fern	*Pteris cretica 'Wilsonii'*
Brazilian edelweiss	*Rechsteineria leucotricha*
Bunny ears	*Opuntia microdasys*
Button fern	*Pellaea rotundifolia*
Calico hearts	*Adromischus maculatus*
Catnip	*Nepeta cataritica*
Chain cactus	*Gymnocalycium mihanovichi*
Chin cactus	*Rhipsalis paradoxa*
Chinese evergreen	*Aglaonema commutatum*
Christmas cheer	*Sedum rubrotinctum*
Cobweb houseleek	*Sempervivum arachnoideum*

Creeping Charlie	*Pilea nummulaeifolia*
Creeping fig	*Ficus pumila*
Crown cactus	*Rebutia kupperiana*
Eyelash begonia	*Begonia boweri*
Fern begonia	*Begonia foliosa*
Fire crown	*Rebutia senilis*
Firefern	*Oxalis hedysaroides*
Flag plant	*Acorus gramineus*
Flaming sword	*Vriesea splendens*
Florist chrysanthemum	*Chrysanthemum frutescens*
German violet	*Exacum affine*
Golden barrel	*Echinocactus grusoni*
Golden thread	*Coptis trifolia*
Gold-eyed aloe	*Aloe nobilis*
Goldfish plant	*Hypocyrta nummularia*
Grape hyacinth	*Muscari aremeniacum*
Grizzly bear	*Opuntia erinacea*
Holly fern	*Cyrtomium falcatum*
Ivy	*Hedera helix*
Jack-in-the-pulpit	*Arisaema triphyllum*
Kenilworth ivy	*Cymbalaria muralis*
Kite orchid	*Masdevallia coccinea*
Kumquat	*Fortunella hindsii*
Lace aloe	*Aloe aristata*
Lace cactus	*Echinocereus reichenbehii*
Lady-of-the-night	*Brassovola nodosa*
Ladyslipper orchid	*Bypripedium parviflorum*
Ladyslipper orchid	*Cypripedium pubescens*
Lemon ball	*Notocactus submannulosus*
Lily-of-the-valley	*Convallaria majalis*
Living stones	*Lithops bella*
Maidenhair fern	*Adiantum cuneatum gracillimum*
Maidenhair spleenwort	*Asplenium trichomanes*
Maple-leaf begonia	*Begonia dregei*
Meadow saffron	*Colchicum bulbocodium*
Mexican firecracker	*Manettia bicolor*
Mexican foxglove	*Allophytum mexicanum*
Mexican snowball	*Echeveria elegans*
Miniature bamboo	*Bambusa nana*
Miniature holly	*Malpighia coccigera*
Mock strawberry	*Fragaria indica*
Moses-in-a-boat	*Rhoeo discolor*
Natal plum	*Carissa grandiflora 'Nana'*
Old lady cactus	*Mammillaria hahniana*

Old man cactus	*Cephalocereus senilis*
Otahetie prange	*Citrus taitensis*
Ox-tongue plant	*Gasteria maculata*
Painted feather	*Vreisea 'Mariae'*
Painted lady	*Echeveria derenbergii*
Panda plant	*Kalenchoe tomemtsa*
Partridge breast aloe	*Aloe variegata*
Peacock plant	*Kaempteria roscoeana*
Peanut cactus	*Chamacereus silvestrii*
Pennywort begonia	*Begonia hydrocotylifolia*
Pincushion cactus	*Mammillaria bocasana*
Pineapple plant	*Eucomis punctata*
Plover eggs	*Adromischus cooperi*
Polka dot plant	*Hypoestes sanquinolata*
Pomegranate	*Punica granatum 'Nana'*
Prayer plant	*Maranata massangeana*
Pussy ears	*Cyanotis somaliense*
Queen's tears	*Billbergia nutans*
Rabbit's foot fern	*Davallia bullata mariesii*
Rattlesnake plant	*Goodyera pubescens*
Rose	*Rosa*
Scarborough lily	*Vallota speciosa*
Scarlet bugler	*Cleistocactus baumannii*
Silver dollar plant	*Crassula arborescens*
Silver beads	*Crassula deltoidea*
Silver torch	*Cleistocactus strausii*
Snowdrops	*Galanthus nivalis*
Spanish shawl	*Schizocentron elegans*
Spleenwort	*Asplenium platyneuron*
Star-of-Bethlehem	*Campanula elatines*
Strawberry geranium	*Saxifraga sarmentosa*
String-of-hearts	*Ceropegia woodii*
Sundew	*Prosera rotundifolia*
Tahitian bridal veil	*Tradescantia mutiflora*
Temple bells	*Smithiantha connabrina*
Tiger's jaws	*Faucaria tigrina*
Tom Thumb cactus	*Parodia aureispina*
Trailing arbutus	*Epigaea repens*
Tulip	*Tulipa*
Venus flytrap	*Dioneae muscipula*
Walking fern	*Camptosorus rhizophyllus*
Watermelon peperomia	*Peperomia sandersii*
Window plant	*Fenestraria aurantiaca*
Window plant	*Fenestraria rhopalophylla*

Wireplant	*Muehleneckia complexa*
Wooly torch	*Cephalocereus palmeri*
Yellow calla-lily	*Zantedeschia elliottiana*

Index